TRICKS AND TREATS

Tricks and Treats

FUN AND EFFECTIVE WAYS TO TRAIN YOUR CAT

Solomon Raj

UNIEK ENTERPRISES

Contents

INDEX

INTRODUCTION

Felines are known for their autonomous and in some cases subtle nature, yet as opposed to mainstream thinking, they can be prepared to perform deceives very much like canines. Preparing animates your catlike companion intellectually as well as fortifies the connection among you and your feline. This guide investigates inventive and charming techniques to prepare your feline, transforming the interaction into a magnificent encounter for both you and your pet.

Figuring out Feline Way of behaving

1.1 The Significance of Preparing for Felines:

In spite of normal discernment, felines can be prepared and partake in the psychological feeling that accompanies it. Preparing gives a potential chance to connect with your feline's regular senses, forestall fatigue, and establish a really improving climate for them. Furthermore, a thoroughly prepared feline is much of the time more happy and less inclined to participate in unwanted ways of behaving.

1.2 Uplifting feedback in Feline Preparation:

Uplifting feedback is the foundation of successful feline preparation. This includes compensating your feline for displaying wanted ways of behaving, empowering them to rehash those activities. Treats, acclaim, or intelligent play meetings can act as successful prizes, making a positive relationship with the ideal way of behaving.

1.3 Figuring out Individual Inclinations:

Each feline is remarkable, with its own arrangement of inclinations and inspirations. A few felines are food-driven, while others answer better to play or love. Noticing your feline's inclinations and fitting your preparation approach appropriately upgrades the odds of coming out on top.

Essential Feline Preparation Orders

2.1 Clicker Preparing for Felines:

Clicker preparing is a well known and viable technique for showing felines new deceives. The clicker fills in as a sign that a prize is coming, definitively denoting the second your feline plays out the ideal way of behaving. After some time, felines figure out how to connect the snap with a positive result.

2.2 Sit and Remain:

Helping your feline to sit and remain on order is a primary expertise. Start by tricking your feline into a sitting situation with a treat, tapping the clicker, and remunerating them.

Bit by bit expand the time your feline remaining parts situated prior to getting the prize.

2.3 High-Five and Paw Shake:

These stunts add a hint of appeal to your feline's collection. Hold a treat over your feline's head, empowering them to raise their paw. As they go after the treat, utilize the clicker and reward them. Rehash until your feline connects the activity with the award.

2.4 Review or Come When Called:

Preparing your feline to come when called isn't just viable yet in addition reinforces your bond. Utilize a particular order, similar to "come" or your feline's name, combined with a treat or toy. Reward your feline each time they answer the order and move toward you.

Advancement Exercises for Mental Feeling

3.1 Riddle Feeders:

Puzzle feeders connect with your feline's critical thinking abilities and give mental feeling. These gadgets apportion treats when controlled accurately, reassuring your feline to think and work for their food. Puzzle feeders come in different plans, from easy to many-sided, taking special care of various ability levels.

3.2 Find the stowaway:

Make a round of find the stowaway by concealing treats or toys around your home. Urge your feline to investigate and find the secret fortunes. This movement takes advantage of their normal hunting senses, keeping them intellectually sharp and actually dynamic.

3.3 Do-It-Yourself Feline Toys and Games:

Making basic Do-It-Yourself toys or games can be a pleasant method for giving mental feeling. Make a hand crafted puzzle feeder utilizing a cardboard box or style a wand play with plumes to draw in your feline in intuitive play. The conceivable outcomes are unfathomable, and the most common way of making toys can be as engaging for you for what it's worth for your feline.

High level Stunts and Spryness Preparing

4.1 Spryness Preparing for Felines:

In all honesty, felines can be prepared to explore spryness courses. Set out a plan with snags like passages, hops, and stages. Urge your feline to explore the course utilizing treats and encouraging feedback. This gives actual activity as well as difficulties their coordination and deftness.

4.2 Twist and Spin:

Helping your feline to turn or spin is an engaging stunt that features their nimbleness. Utilize a treat to direct your feline in a roundabout movement, steadily expanding the twist. Snap and prize when your feline finishes the revolution. With persistence, your feline can figure out how to turn on order.

4.3 Get:

While usually connected with canines, a few felines can be prepared to get. Begin with a most loved toy, tenderly throw it, and urge your feline to take it back to you. Utilize uplifting feedback to compensate each effective recovery. Get gives active work as well as fortifies the connection among you and your catlike companion.

Beating Difficulties in Feline Preparation

5.1 Tolerance and Consistency:

Preparing a feline requires tolerance and consistency. Felines may not get a handle on orders right away, so it's fundamental to stay patient and rehash instructional courses consistently. Consistency in orders, rewards, and the utilization of encouraging feedback is critical for effective preparation.

5.2 Perceiving Restrictions:

It's fundamental to perceive that not all felines will succeed in each stunt or movement. Each feline has its own character, and some might be more responsive to preparing than others. Be sensitive to your feline's solace level and change your assumptions in like manner.

5.3 Resolving Conduct Issues:

In the event that your feline showcases social issues during preparing, for example, dread or hostility, tending to these concerns is urgent. Talk with a veterinarian or an expert creature behaviorist to recognize the underlying driver and foster a custom-made preparing plan.

1. The Healing Power of Cats

The friendship among people and felines has risen above simple living together, developing into an interesting and restorative bond. Past the perky tricks and relieving murmurs, felines have been perceived for their significant mending skills, adding to the physical, mental, and profound prosperity of their human partners. This far reaching investigation digs into the complex parts of the recuperating force of felines, revealing insight into the restorative advantages they bring to our lives.

The Actual Medical advantages

1.1 Pressure Decrease:

Felines have a natural capacity to give solace and lighten pressure. The demonstration of petting a feline triggers the arrival of oxytocin, the "vibe great" chemical, prompting a diminishing in feelings of anxiety. The cadenced murmuring of a feline affects the sensory system, advancing unwinding and diminishing tension.

1.2 Bringing down Pulse:

Studies have shown that possessing a feline can add to bring down pulse. The quieting presence of a feline, joined with the demonstration of petting, emphatically affects cardiovascular wellbeing. This regular pressure decrease can add to a better heart and generally prosperity.

1.3 Agony The executives:

Feline treatment has been investigated in different clinical settings to oversee torment. The friendship of a feline can divert people from actual distress, and the demonstration of petting has been related with the arrival of endorphins, the body's regular pain killers.

1.4 Superior Rest Quality:

The quieting presence of a feline in the room can add to further developed rest quality. The cadenced murmuring and delicate warmth give a feeling that everything is good, helping people unwind and accomplish better rest designs. Felines' rest propensities can likewise impact their proprietors to lay out better rest schedules.

Mental and Profound Prosperity

2.1 Mitigating Melancholy and Tension:

Felines assume a fundamental part in easing side effects of melancholy and uneasiness. The friendship they offer makes a feeling of direction and schedule. The demonstration of really focusing on a feline, including taking care of, prepping, and play, can give a construction that assists people with defeating the difficulties of psychological wellness problems.

2.2 Friendship for the Old:

Felines are much of the time astounding allies for the older, offering actual solace as well as mitigating sensations of depression and detachment. The presence of a feline gives a wellspring of connection and love, adding to worked on mental prosperity in more seasoned people.

2.3 Basic reassurance Creatures:

Felines are progressively perceived as basic reassurance creatures (ESAs) because of their capacity to give solace and friendship. For people confronting inner difficulties, having a feline as an ESA can offer a remedial presence, encouraging close to home soundness and flexibility.

2.4 Decreasing Sensations of Confinement:

Particularly in the present quick moving, carefully associated world, people might encounter sensations of separation. Felines, with their free yet warm nature, can overcome any barrier, giving a wellspring of association and lessening the feeling of forlornness that can add to psychological well-being issues.

Felines in Helpful Settings

3.1 Creature Helped Treatment:

Felines assume a critical part in creature helped treatment (AAT), a type of treatment that integrates creatures into the remedial cycle. In medical services settings, schools, and restoration focuses, felines are utilized to give solace, friendship, and basic reassurance to people going through different therapies.

3.2 Felines in Hospice Care:

The mitigating presence of felines is progressively being incorporated into hospice care programs. Felines offer solace and comfort to people confronting terminal diseases, giving a wellspring of friendship during testing times. Their natural nature permits them to offer an extraordinary type of help in these delicate settings.

3.3 Restoration and Recuperation:

In restoration habitats, felines add to the recuperation cycle of people managing actual wounds or psychological wellness challenges. The presence of a feline can spur patients to participate in exercises, giving a positive interruption and encouraging a feeling of direction during the mending venture.

The Helpful Connection Among Felines and Youngsters

4.1 Mental imbalance Range Issue:

For youngsters with mental imbalance range jumble (ASD), the friendship of a feline can be especially valuable. Felines' quiet disposition and unsurprising ways of behaving can establish a consoling climate, assisting kids with ASD oversee tangible responsive qualities and social communications.

4.2 Profound Guideline:

Felines can support profound guideline for youngsters confronting social or inner difficulties. The non-critical and tolerating nature of felines permits youngsters to articulate their thoughts uninhibitedly, adding to the advancement of the ability to appreciate anyone on a deeper level and survival techniques.

4.3 Instructing Liability:

Really focusing on a feline shows kids important fundamental abilities, including liability and compassion. Taking care of, preparing, and playing with a feline ingrain a feeling of routine and responsibility, cultivating a kid's personal and mental turn of events.

The Extraordinary Characteristics of Felines in Recuperating

5.1 Natural Friendship:

Felines have a natural sense that permits them to get on their proprietor's feelings. They frequently answer human trouble with consoling ways of behaving, like sitting on an individual's lap or delicately pushing them, giving a one of a kind type of basic encouragement.

5.2 Non-Critical Presence:

Felines are known for their non-critical and tolerating nature. This genuine acknowledgment makes a place of refuge for people to act naturally, cultivating a feeling of having a place and lessening the apprehension about judgment that can be a hindrance to looking for help.

5.3 Intergenerational Association:

Felines have the ability to surprise to associate with people, everything being equal. Whether it's a youngster, a grown-up, or an old individual, the presence of a feline can make a common encounter that rises above generational limits, advancing a feeling of solidarity and interconnectedness.

Reasonable Methods for Integrating Felines into Mending

6.1 Taking on a Sanctuary Feline:

The recuperating force of felines isn't restricted to families. Many felines in covers are needing adoring homes and can offer similar restorative advantages as some other feline. Taking on a sanctuary feline not just gives a home to a meriting creature yet additionally carries the potential for significant mending to the adopter.

6.2 Establishing a Climate that welcomes felines:

Guaranteeing that your house is feline well disposed is urgent for boosting the restorative advantages of cat friendship. This incorporates giving an agreeable and place of refuge, participating in intelligent play, and offering valuable open doors for mental feeling through toys and improvement exercises.

6.3 Customary Veterinary Consideration:

Keeping up with your feline's wellbeing is fundamental for guaranteeing a positive and helpful relationship. Standard veterinary check-ups, legitimate nourishment, and regard for prepping add to a sound and cheerful feline, upgrading the general prosperity of both the feline and its proprietor.

1. **Therapeutic Benefits**

   The idea of treatment stretches out a long ways past conventional clinical settings, including a wide range of approaches that add to physical, mental, and profound prosperity. This thorough investigation dives into the multi-layered restorative advantages across different spaces, from regular remedial intercessions to elective works on, featuring the interconnectedness of these methodologies and their aggregate effect on comprehensive wellbeing.

Conventional Treatments

1.1 Psychotherapy:

Psychotherapy, frequently alluded to as talk treatment, is a foundation of conventional psychological well-being treatment. Different modalities, including mental conduct treatment (CBT), psychoanalytic treatment, and humanistic treatment, intend to resolve mental issues, work on profound prosperity, and improve survival strategies. The helpful relationship framed between the client and specialist encourages a place of refuge for self-investigation and development.

1.2 Exercise based recuperation:

Exercise based recuperation is a urgent part of restoration and recuperation for people managing actual wounds, persistent circumstances, or post-careful intercessions. Advisors utilize designated works out, manual strategies, and different modalities to further develop versatility, decrease torment, and re-establish useful freedom. The cooperative idea of exercise based recuperation enables people to take part in their mending cycle effectively.

1.3 Word related Treatment:

Word related treatment centers around working on people's capacity to perform everyday exercises and take part in significant life jobs. Advisors work with clients to foster abilities, adjust conditions, and advance freedom, especially for those with inabilities or recuperating from wounds. The all encompassing methodology of word related treatment considers the physical, mental, and profound parts of prosperity.

1.4 Language instruction:

Language instruction tends to correspondence and gulping problems, incorporating a scope of conditions from discourse obstructions to language improvement issues. Advisors utilize activities, methods, and assistive gadgets to upgrade relational abilities and work on generally speaking personal satisfaction for people confronting discourse related difficulties.

Integrative Treatments

2.1 Craftsmanship Treatment:

Craftsmanship treatment tackles the innovative flow to work on mental and close to home prosperity. Through different fine arts, people can put themselves out there, investigate feelings, and gain bits of knowledge into their viewpoints and sentiments. This non-verbal way to deal with treatment is especially valuable for the individuals who might find conventional talk treatment testing.

2.2 Music Treatment:

Music treatment uses the force of music to address close to home, mental, and actual requirements. Board-guaranteed music advisors work with clients to take part in exercises like singing, tuning in, and making music, advancing unwinding, self-articulation, and close to home guideline. Music treatment is applied in different settings, from psychological well-being offices to restoration focuses.

2.3 Dance/Development Treatment:

Dance/development treatment perceives the brain body association and utilizes development as an instrument for self-articulation and recuperating. Specialists guide people through development activities to investigate feelings, further develop body mindfulness, and upgrade by and large prosperity. This exemplified approach is especially viable in tending to injury and stress-related messes.

2.4 Creature Helped Treatment:

Creature helped treatment integrates creatures into the restorative cycle to accomplish explicit treatment objectives. Communications with treatment creatures, like canines or ponies, can decrease pressure, further develop state of mind, and upgrade social associations. This approach is especially successful in emotional wellness settings, recovery focuses, and custom curriculum programs.

Nature-Based Treatments

3.1 Ecotherapy:

Ecotherapy, otherwise called nature treatment, perceives the mending force of the common habitat. Remedial mediations happen outside, connecting with people in exercises like climbing, cultivating, or basically investing energy in nature. Ecotherapy advances mental prosperity, diminishes pressure, and cultivates a feeling of association with the climate.

3.2 Woodland Washing:

Beginning from Japanese practices, woods washing, or shinrin-yoku, includes submerging oneself in a backwoods climate to encounter the remedial advantages of nature. This training has been related with diminished pressure, further developed temperament, and improved safe capability. Timberland washing underscores careful presence in regular environmental factors.

3.3 Plant Treatment:

Green treatment uses cultivating and plant-related exercises to advance physical, mental, and close to home prosperity. Taking part in cultivating undertakings, from sowing seeds to tending to plants, offers helpful advantages like pressure decrease, further developed mind-set, and expanded confidence. Green treatment is applied in various settings, including recovery focuses and emotional wellness offices.

Mind-Body Practices

4.1 Contemplation and Care:

Contemplation and care rehearses include developing present-second mindfulness and encouraging a non-critical mentality toward considerations and sentiments. These practices, established in antiquated customs, have been integrated into current restorative methodologies. Care based mediations are successful in decreasing pressure, uneasiness, and advancing by and large mental prosperity.

4.2 Yoga Treatment:

Yoga treatment consolidates actual stances, breathwork, and reflection to address physical and psychological well-being issues. Custom fitted to individual necessities, yoga treatment advances adaptability, strength, and unwinding. It has been used as a corresponding methodology in the therapy of conditions like persistent torment, uneasiness, and wretchedness.

4.3 Kendo:

Kendo is a brain body practice that started in old China and includes slow, streaming developments and profound relaxing. This reflective military workmanship advances equilibrium, adaptability, and unwinding. Jujitsu has been displayed to have helpful advantages for conditions like joint inflammation, hypertension, and stress-related messes.

4.4 Biofeedback:

Biofeedback is a remedial method that empowers people to oversee physiological cycles, for example, pulse, muscle pressure, and skin temperature. By giving ongoing criticism, people figure out how to control these cycles, prompting further developed pressure the board and by and large prosperity.

Helpful Advantages in Unambiguous Populaces

5.1 Youngsters and Teenagers:

Helpful intercessions for youngsters and youths frequently include play treatment, workmanship treatment, and exercises that work with self-articulation. These methodologies assist youngsters with exploring personal difficulties, fabricate versatility, and foster fundamental adapting abilities. Play-based treatments establish a harmless climate for youthful people to investigate their feelings.

5.2 More seasoned Grown-ups:

Restorative mediations for more established grown-ups center around keeping up with mental capability, actual wellbeing, and close to home prosperity. Exercises like memory treatment, workmanship treatment, and actual activities add to mental feeling, close to home articulation, and in general personal satisfaction for more established people.

5.3 People with Incapacities:

Remedial intercessions for people with handicaps are custom-made to address explicit necessities and difficulties. Word related treatment, exercise based recuperation, and imaginative treatments assume a urgent part in advancing freedom, further developing versatility, and improving the general personal satisfaction for people with different capacities.

5.4 Veterans and Injury Survivors:

Veterans and injury survivors frequently benefit from specific helpful mediations that address post-awful pressure issue (PTSD) and related difficulties. Approaches like eye development desensitization and going back over (EMDR), equine treatment, and gathering treatment offer help and recuperating in the result of injury.

Difficulties and Contemplations in Treatment

6.1 Social Awareness:

Social awareness is fundamental in treatment to guarantee that mediations are comprehensive and deferential of assorted foundations. Advisors should be sensitive to social subtleties, conviction frameworks, and practices to give viable and socially capable consideration.

6.2 Availability:

Admittance to remedial mediations stays a critical test for some people. Financial variables, geological area, and disgrace can go about as hindrances to looking for and getting treatment. Endeavors to increment availability through telehealth, local area based administrations, and mindfulness crusades are critical in tending to this test.

6.3 Personalization of Treatment:

One size doesn't fit all in treatment. Personalization is vital to successful remedial intercessions. Fitting ways to deal with individual requirements, inclinations, and social settings improves the probability of progress in accomplishing helpful objectives.

6.4 Integrative Methodologies:

Cooperation among different restorative modalities is known as integrative treatment. Consolidating customary treatments with option or correlative methodologies gives an all encompassing and customized treatment plan. Integrative methodologies consider the interconnectedness of physical, mental, and close to home prosperity.

2. Emotional Support

In the unpredictable embroidery of human life, consistent reassurance arises as a crucial string that winds through the texture of our prosperity. Characterized as the arrangement of solace, understanding, and consolation to somebody in the midst of stress or trouble, daily encouragement assumes a critical part in cultivating emotional well-being and strength. This extensive investigation will dig into the different components of consistent reassurance, its importance, and the significant effect it can have on people exploring the intricacies of life.

Grasping Daily encouragement

Consistent encouragement envelops an expansive range of activities, articulations, and ways of behaving that convey sympathy and empathy. It goes past simple compassion, developing into a powerful power that supports people during testing times. This help can be verbal, non-verbal, or even exhibited through activities, all with the normal point of reducing close to home misery and giving a feeling of association.

Verbal articulations of help might incorporate empowering words, undivided attention, and attestations. Non-verbal help can appear through motions, like a consoling touch, a warm hug, or essentially being available. Activities, in the mean time, may include functional help, such as assisting with day to day errands or offering some assistance in the midst of emergency.

Meaning of Consistent reassurance

Emotional wellness and Close to home Prosperity:

Consistent reassurance fills in as a foundation for emotional wellness, offering comfort during snapshots of nervousness, sadness, or overpowering pressure. Concentrates reliably feature the positive connection between's consistent reassurance and mental prosperity, underlining its job in forestalling the beginning of emotional wellness issues and advancing mental versatility.

Building Strength:

Strength, the capacity to quickly return from misfortune, is a characteristic sustained by consistent reassurance. At the point when people feel upheld, they are better outfitted to adapt to life's difficulties. This versatility supports defeating misfortunes as well as works with self-improvement and advancement.

Upgraded Survival strategies:

The presence of everyday reassurance improves a singular's survival strategies. Realizing that there is an organization of individuals who grasp, care, and deal unqualified help enables people to stand up to troubles with a more sure outlook, diminishing the profound cost of misfortune.

Reinforcing Relational Bonds:

Daily encouragement cultivates further associations between people. At the point when individuals feel upheld, trust and closeness thrive, making a good criticism circle that reinforces connections. This enhances unique interactions as well as adds to a more extensive feeling of local area and social prosperity.

Kinds of Basic encouragement

Instrumental Help:

This type of help includes substantial help with the type of assets, time, or activities. It very well may be essentially as basic as assisting with family errands, giving monetary help, or effectively partaking in critical thinking. Instrumental help tends to down to earth needs, supporting the thought that activities can express stronger than words.

Close to home Approval:

In some cases, people look for approval of their feelings and encounters. Basic encouragement that includes recognizing and approving sentiments contributes fundamentally to a person's close to home prosperity. This approval makes a place of refuge for communicating feelings unafraid of judgment.

Enlightening Help:

During a time of data, knowing where to go for direction is significant. Instructive help includes giving information, exhortation, or direction to assist people with exploring difficulties. This kind of help can engage people to pursue informed choices and feel more in charge of their conditions.

Friendship:

Dejection and confinement can intensify profound misery. Friendship, through getting to know each other, participating in shared exercises, or basically being available, addresses the human requirement for association. Such help can be particularly crucial during seasons of misery, misfortune, or significant life advances.

The Job of Consistent encouragement in Different Life Stages

Youth and Puberty:

Daily encouragement during youth and puberty establishes the groundwork for sound profound turn of events. Parental help, specifically, shapes a kid's feeling that all is well with the world, self-esteem, and capacity to frame sound connections. Peer support additionally turns out to be progressively significant during youthfulness as people explore character development and social difficulties.

Adulthood:

In adulthood, the requirement for daily reassurance continues and develops. Associations with significant others, companions, and partners become focal wellsprings of help. As people face the intricacies of work, family, and self-improvement, the job of daily reassurance in moderating pressure and advancing prosperity stays critical.

More seasoned Adulthood:

As people age, the meaning of consistent encouragement becomes articulated. More seasoned grown-ups may confront issues, for example, wellbeing concerns, loss of friends and family, and advances into retirement. The presence of a steady organization turns into a cradle against the possible adverse consequences of these life altering events, advancing a more certain and satisfying later life.

Hindrances to Daily encouragement

Regardless of its significance, daily encouragement can confront different boundaries that thwart its compelling arrangement:

Disgrace Encompassing Psychological well-being:

Cultural disgrace connected with psychological well-being issues can deter people from looking for or offering consistent reassurance. Apprehension about judgment or segregation might lead individuals to experience peacefully, building up the significance of encouraging open discussions around emotional wellness.

Absence of Relational abilities:

Compelling basic reassurance frequently requires solid relational abilities. Not every person has the capacity to communicate compassion, effectively tune in, or explore genuinely charged discussions. Putting resources into relational abilities preparing can upgrade the nature of consistent encouragement gave.

Social and Orientation Standards:

Social and orientation standards can impact how daily encouragement is seen and communicated. In certain societies, looking for daily encouragement might be trashed, while orientation standards might direct unambiguous jobs and assumptions for close to home articulation. Perceiving and testing these standards is fundamental for cultivating a more comprehensive and strong climate.

Advanced Age Difficulties:

The ascent of advanced correspondence, while giving new roads to association, can likewise present difficulties to genuine daily encouragement. Shallow associations via web-based entertainment might supplant further, eye to eye associations. Adjusting the advantages of innovation with the requirement for authentic human association is vital in the computerized age.

Advancing a Culture of Daily encouragement

Instructive Drives:

Incorporating the capacity to understand anyone on a profound level and relational abilities into instructive educational plans can enable people to explore connections and proposition viable daily reassurance. Instructive drives can likewise assist with decreasing the shame related with looking for help for psychological wellness concerns.

Working environment Backing Projects:

The work environment is a critical climate where basic encouragement can have a significant effect. Executing worker help programs, advancing a culture of sympathy, and giving assets to psychological well-being backing can add to a better and more useful labor force.

Local area Commitment:

Building a feeling of local area includes cultivating associations past individual connections. Local area commitment drives, support gatherings, and psychological well-being mindfulness crusades add to establishing conditions where everyday reassurance is both esteemed and promptly accessible.

Media Portrayal:

Media assumes a strong part in molding cultural perspectives. Addressing different stories of basic encouragement in media can challenge generalizations and standardize the significance of looking for and offering help. This can add to a social shift towards more prominent transparency about emotional wellness.

Chapter 1

Becoming A Therapy Cat Trainer

Turning into a treatment feline coach is a fulfilling and interesting profession way that consolidates an adoration for cats enthusiastically for helping other people. Treatment felines assume a critical part in giving solace and backing to people in different settings, including clinics, nursing homes, and schools. In this extensive aide, we will investigate the excursion to turning into a treatment feline mentor, from understanding the job and significance of treatment felines to the abilities and preparing expected for both the felines and their coaches.

Understanding the Job of Treatment Felines:

Treatment felines are exceptionally prepared cats that offer basic encouragement to individuals out of luck. Dissimilar to support creatures, treatment felines are not prepared for explicit assignments but instead for giving friendship and solace. They can be utilized in different conditions, from clinical offices to catastrophe reaction circumstances. The positive effect of treatment felines on mental and profound prosperity has prompted an expanded interest for qualified mentors in this field.

Characteristics of a Fruitful Treatment Feline Mentor:

Turning into a treatment feline mentor requires a special arrangement of abilities and characteristics. Tolerance, sympathy, and a profound comprehension of cat conduct are fundamental. Mentors ought to likewise have magnificent relational abilities to work really with the two felines and their proprietors. Adaptability and flexibility are significant while managing various characters, both catlike and human, as each feline has its own personality and learning pace.

Instructive Foundation and Preparing:

While there is no particular instructive way to turning into a treatment feline coach, a foundation in creature science, brain research, or a connected field can be favorable. Moreover, acquiring affirmation from perceived associations, like the Global Relationship of Canine Experts (IACP), can upgrade validity. Useful experience is similarly vital, and hopeful coaches frequently volunteer or work with laid out treatment feline projects to acquire involved preparing.

Building Areas of strength for an in Cat Conduct:

Understanding cat conduct is at the center of treatment feline preparation. Mentors should be knowledgeable in feline non-verbal communication, correspondence signals, and the brain research behind their activities. This information empowers coaches to distinguish pressure, dread, or distress in treatment felines and address these issues really. Building major areas of strength for an in cat conduct is a continuous cycle, including nonstop learning and remaining refreshed on the most recent examination in feline brain science.

Preparing Strategies for Treatment Felines:

Preparing treatment felines includes a mix of uplifting feedback, socialization, and desensitization strategies. Felines ought to be presented to different conditions, sounds, and individuals to guarantee they keep quiet and created in assorted settings. Encouraging feedback, like treats or recognition, is utilized to support wanted ways of behaving. It's fundamental for mentors to be patient and versatile, perceiving that each feline advances at its own speed.

Making Individualized Preparing Plans:

Every treatment feline is one of a kind, and making individualized preparing plans is critical to progress. Coaches survey the feline's character, energy levels, and solace with different improvements to tailor a program that suits the particular requirements of the feline and the climate it will work in. Factors like age, wellbeing, and past encounters additionally impact the preparation approach. The capacity to tweak preparing plans features the coach's skill in perceiving and tending to individual contrasts.

Working with Feline Proprietors:

Treatment feline coaches frequently work intimately with the proprietors of the treatment felines. This coordinated effort is essential in guaranteeing a durable and fruitful preparation experience. Coaches teach proprietors about cat conduct, offer direction on building up sure ways of behaving at home, and offer help in dealing with likely difficulties. Compelling correspondence with feline proprietors encourages a confiding in relationship and upgrades the general prosperity of the treatment feline.

Affirmations and Certification:

While there is no all inclusive confirmation for treatment feline mentors, getting license from respectable associations adds believability to one's ability. The Worldwide Relationship of Cat Experts (IAFP) and the American Relationship of Expert Feline Coaches (AAPCT) are instances of associations that offer affirmations and progressing proficient advancement potential open doors for people in the field. Accomplishing certificate exhibits a guarantee to greatness and adherence to industry guidelines.

Acquiring Pragmatic Experience:

Reasonable experience is significant in the excursion to turning into a capable treatment feline coach. This can be procured through chipping in at creature covers, partaking in treatment creature projects, or working under the direction of experienced coaches. Involved experience permits hopeful coaches to apply hypothetical information, improve their useful abilities, and fabricate major areas of strength for an inside the expert local area.

Building an Expert Organization:

Building associations inside the business is urgent for remaining informed about the most recent patterns, examination, and valuable open doors. Going to gatherings, studios, and systems administration occasions permits treatment feline coaches to trade thoughts, team up on projects, and gain from experienced experts. A hearty expert organization works with consistent advancing as well as opens ways to possible clients, joint efforts, and professional success.

Moral Contemplations in Treatment Feline Preparation:

Moral contemplations are foremost in the field of treatment feline preparation. Coaches should focus on the prosperity of the felines and guarantee their preparation strategies line up with moral norms. This incorporates keeping away from any type of compulsion or discipline and continuously focusing on the solace and satisfaction of the treatment felines. Moral practices construct entrust with clients and add to the positive standing of the mentor inside the local area.

Challenges in Treatment Feline Preparation:

While the prizes of treatment feline preparation are various, there are likewise difficulties to explore. Felines, being free animals, may not necessarily in all cases answer typically to preparing endeavors. Mentors should be ready to adjust their techniques, address startling ways of behaving, and work cooperatively with proprietors to conquer difficulties. Moreover, overseeing client assumptions and teaching them about the reasonable results of treatment feline preparation is fundamental for a fruitful organization.

Keeping up with Proceeded with Proficient Turn of events:

The field of treatment feline preparation is dynamic, with continuous examination and developing prescribed procedures. Hopeful mentors and old pros the same should resolve to proceeded with proficient improvement to keep up to date with new data, methods, and innovations. Participating in online classes, going to gatherings, and partaking in cutting edge preparing programs add to the continuous development and greatness of treatment feline mentors.

Potential Vocation Ways for Treatment Feline Mentors:

Treatment feline coaches have different profession ways accessible to them. They might decide to work autonomously, offering private preparation administrations to people and associations. On the other hand, they can work together with laid out treatment creature programs, medical care offices, or schools. A few coaches might have practical experience in working with explicit populaces, like youngsters, the old, or people with exceptional necessities. The flexibility of the calling permits mentors to cut a specialty that lines up with their enthusiasm and skill.

1. Understanding the Requirements

In the domain of venture the board and programming advancement, one of the central advances is the reasonable and far reaching comprehension of necessities. The progress of any task depends on the capacity to accumulate, investigate, and report prerequisites actually. This cycle makes way for the whole task lifecycle, impacting all that from plan and advancement to testing and execution. In this broad aide, we will dig into the different parts of understanding prerequisites, investigating why it is significant, the systems utilized, normal difficulties confronted, and best practices for guaranteeing fruitful necessity the executives.

1. Significance of Figuring out Prerequisites

1.1. Underpinning of Venture Achievement

At the center of any effective task lies an intensive comprehension of prerequisites. Necessities act as the extension between the client's assumptions and the task group's expectations. Neglecting to grasp the client's requirements can bring about misalignment, expanded project costs, and eventually project disappointment. Consequently, the capacity to precisely catch and decipher necessities is an essential expertise for project supervisors and colleagues the same.

1.2. Upgrading Correspondence

Prerequisites go about as a specialized instrument between partners, including clients, project supervisors, designers, and analyzers. An unmistakable and unambiguous comprehension of necessities guarantees that everybody engaged with the undertaking is in total agreement. Viable correspondence of necessities forestalls errors, diminishes the probability of improve, and cultivates a cooperative climate.

1.3. Moderating Dangers

Insufficient necessity investigation can prompt undertaking dangers, for example, project requirements getting out of control, financial plan overwhelms, and missed cutoff times.

By putting time and exertion in understanding prerequisites completely, project administrators can recognize potential dangers right off the bat in the undertaking lifecycle and execute procedures to moderate them. This proactive methodology adds to smoother project execution and expanded odds of coming out on top.

2. Philosophies for Necessity Social affair and Examination

2.1. Conventional Methodologies

All things considered, projects have utilized customary prerequisite social event strategies, like meetings, overviews, and archive audits. While these strategies give significant experiences, they can be tedious and may not catch advancing necessities really. Moreover, depending exclusively on customary methodologies might bring about missed subtleties and changes in client assumptions.

2.2. Deft Strategies

Coordinated strategies, including Scrum and Kanban, have acquired notoriety for their adaptability and iterative methodology. In a Nimble climate, necessities are frequently assembled gradually and advance all through the venture. Client stories, excess preparing, and run arranging are normal practices that add to a dynamic and responsive necessity the board interaction. Light-footed systems are especially powerful for projects where prerequisites are supposed to as often as possible change.

2.3. Prototyping and Mockups

Making models and mockups is a visual and unmistakable method for understanding and approve necessities. These portrayals furnish partners with a substantial perception of the finished result, assisting with uncovering potential misconceptions from the get-go in the improvement cycle. Prototyping is particularly gainful for projects with a huge UI part, permitting clients to communicate with a visual portrayal of the item before improvement starts.

3. Challenges in Figuring out Prerequisites

3.1. Equivocalness and Vulnerability

One of the essential difficulties in necessity the executives is managing equivocal or unsure prerequisites. Clients may not generally express their requirements plainly, prompting misconceptions and misinterpretations. Project groups should utilize powerful correspondence methodologies, like explaining prerequisites through conversations and documentation, to address equivocalness and decrease vulnerability.

3.2. Changing Necessities

In powerful conditions, necessities are inclined to change due to advancing business needs, market patterns, or unexpected difficulties. Overseeing changing prerequisites requires an adaptable methodology and the capacity to rapidly adjust. Dexterous systems, with their iterative and gradual nature, are appropriate to deal with evolving necessities, however they require a mentality shift and nonstop correspondence between the undertaking group and partners.

3.3. Partner Arrangement

Partners might have different assumptions and needs, prompting clashing necessities. It is pivotal to effectively draw in with partners, guaranteeing their arrangement on project objectives and goals. Normal correspondence channels, for example, status gatherings and progress refreshes, assist with keeping a mutual perspective among all gatherings included.

4. **Best Practices for Prerequisite Administration**

4.1. Draw in Partners Early and Frequently

Fruitful prerequisite administration begins with dynamic and constant commitment with partners. Early inclusion permits project groups to acquire a profound comprehension of client assumptions and works with the structure major areas of strength for of. Normal collaborations all through the venture lifecycle guarantee that any progressions in prerequisites are recognized and tended to immediately.

4.2. Utilize an Organized Necessities Documentation Cycle

Reporting prerequisites in an organized and coordinated way is fundamental for lucidity and detectability. Utilizing a normalized layout for prerequisites documentation guarantees consistency and empowers simple reference during various venture stages. Key parts of a necessities report might incorporate a portrayal of the prerequisite, acknowledgment measures, and any conditions.

4.3. Carry out Powerful Correspondence Channels

Laying out clear and open correspondence channels is vital for understanding and overseeing prerequisites really. Normal gatherings, announcements, and cooperative apparatuses can work with correspondence among colleagues and partners. Furthermore, making a criticism circle for prerequisites approval guarantees that any misconceptions are distinguished early and tended to expeditiously.

4.4. Influence Prototyping and Representation Methods

Picturing prerequisites through models, mockups, or wireframes is a strong method for upgrading understanding. These visual portrayals furnish partners with a substantial review of the finished result, permitting them to approve and give input on the plan and usefulness. Prototyping can be particularly gainful for projects where client experience is a basic element.

4.5. Utilize Iterative Methodologies

Consolidating iterative methodologies, like those tracked down in Light-footed procedures, considers nonstop refinement of necessities all through the undertaking. Consistently checking on and adjusting necessities in view of criticism and changing conditions forestalls misconceptions and guarantees that the last deliverable adjusts intimately with the client's assumptions.

4.6. Direct Standard Necessity Audits and Investigations

Occasional surveys and examinations of prerequisites with key partners assist with distinguishing any disparities, holes, or changes from the get-go in the task. This cooperative methodology guarantees that everybody in question has a mutual perspective of the necessities and diminishes the probability of significant modifications later in the improvement cycle.

5. **Contextual analyses in Prerequisite Administration**

5.1. The Fruitful Execution of Spry in Programming Improvement

This contextual investigation investigates how an association effectively changed from a conventional cascade model to a Coordinated improvement approach. By taking on Dexterous systems, the association worked on its capacity to comprehend and answer evolving prerequisites, bringing about quicker time-to-showcase and expanded client fulfillment.

5.2. Illustrations Gained from Necessity The board Disappointments

Looking at occurrences of prerequisite administration disappointments gives important bits of knowledge into the results of ignoring this basic part of task the board. This contextual investigation examines projects that confronted difficulties because of unfortunate prerequisite comprehension, underscoring the significance of strong necessity social occasion and examination processes.

6. **Future Patterns in Necessity The board**

6.1. Man-made reasoning and Robotization

The combination of man-made brainpower (simulated intelligence) and mechanization apparatuses in prerequisite administration is ready to change the manner in which tasks accumulate, examine, and oversee necessities. Artificial intelligence calculations can help with distinguishing designs, anticipating expected issues, and robotizing routine assignments, opening up project groups to zero in on additional complicated parts of prerequisite examination.

6.2. Blockchain for Detectability and Straightforwardness

Blockchain innovation offers the possibility to upgrade discernibility and straightforwardness in necessity the executives. By utilizing blockchain, project groups can make a safe and sealed record of prerequisite changes, guaranteeing a straightforward and auditable path. This can be especially important in ventures with rigid consistence necessities.

6.3. Consistent Criticism Circles

As associations progressively embrace a culture of constant improvement, ceaseless criticism circles in necessity the executives will turn out to be more common. Ongoing criticism instruments, combined with information investigation, empower project groups to adjust to changing necessities quickly and upgrade generally speaking undertaking results.

1. **Temperament and Personality Traits**

The investigation of disposition and character qualities has been a longstanding undertaking in brain research, planning to unwind the mind boggling transaction of variables that shape human way of behaving, feelings, and points of view. Both disposition and character are vital parts of a person's mental cosmetics, impacting how they associate with the world, answer difficulties, and structure connections. In this thorough investigation, we will dig into the definitions, hypotheses, and estimation of demeanor and character attributes, analyzing their effect on different parts of human existence.

1. **Figuring out Demeanor**

   1.1. Meaning of Demeanor

   Demeanor alludes to the natural, organically based part of a singular's character that arises right off the bat throughout everyday life and remains generally stable over the long haul. It incorporates conduct propensities, close to home reactivity, and generally mind-set.

   Demeanor is in many cases considered the establishment whereupon more complicated character qualities are constructed, giving a benchmark to understanding a singular's trademark examples of answering upgrades.

   1.2. Verifiable Viewpoints on Demeanor

   The investigation of personality can be followed back to old Greece, where early logicians, for example, Hippocrates proposed the presence of four basic dispositions: optimistic, irritable, melancholic, and indifferent. These arrangements depended on the conviction that natural liquids, or "humors," impacted character qualities. While contemporary brain research has gotten away from such physiological clarifications, the center thought that people have intrinsic and unmistakable touchy characteristics stays pertinent.

   1.3. Present day Ways to deal with Personality

   Contemporary points of view on disposition draw on a blend of hereditary, neurological, and natural variables. Clinicians, like Alexander Thomas and Stella Chess, have contributed altogether to the advanced comprehension of personality. They recognized nine elements of disposition, including action level, rhythmicity, approach/withdrawal, versatility, force of response, limit of responsiveness, nature of state of mind, distractibility, and capacity to focus/perseverance.

2. **Character Attributes: The Large Five**

   2.1. The Five-Component Model

   Character qualities, then again, are more extensive examples of conduct, feeling, and perception that portray a person across different circumstances. One of the most broadly acknowledged models for understanding character qualities is the Five-Variable Model (FFM), otherwise called the Large Five. The Large Five involves five wide aspects: receptiveness to encounter, good faith, extraversion, appropriateness, and neuroticism (Sea). Each aspect addresses a range along which people differ, adding to the uniqueness of their character.

2.2. Receptiveness to Experience

Receptiveness to encounter mirrors how much people are liberal, inquisitive, and responsive to novel thoughts, encounters, and difficulties. Those high in transparency will quite often be innovative, creative, and open to whimsical considerations, while people low in receptiveness might favor routine and commonality.

2.3. Reliability

Reliability alludes to the degree to which people are coordinated, mindful, and objective arranged. Exceptionally principled people are frequently solid, persistent, and restrained, while those low in honesty might battle with impulsivity and an absence of long haul arranging.

2.4. Extraversion

Extraversion addresses how much people are friendly, agreeable, and vigorous. Extraverts flourish in friendly circumstances, look for feeling, and are by and large self-assured, while contemplative people will quite often be more saved, intelligent, and favor singular exercises.

2.5. Pleasantness

Pleasantness mirrors the degree to which people are helpful, merciful, and thoughtful. Profoundly pleasing people are compassionate and esteem relational amicability, while those low in appropriateness might be more cutthroat or doubtful.

2.6. Neuroticism

Neuroticism, otherwise called close to home soundness, gauges the level of profound precariousness and reactivity to push. People high in neuroticism might be inclined to tension, temperament swings, and weakness, while those low in neuroticism are all the more sincerely strong and calm.

3. **Disposition and Character Advancement**

3.1. Youth Starting points

Disposition establishes the groundwork for the improvement of character qualities, with youth encounters assuming a critical part. Research shows that specific unpredictable qualities displayed in early stages, like reactivity and flexibility, can foresee the development of explicit character attributes further down the road. For instance, a kid who is exceptionally receptive and effortlessly resentful might be more inclined to foster neuroticism as a character quality.

3.2. Natural Impacts

While demeanor has areas of strength for a premise, ecological factors likewise contribute fundamentally to the improvement of character. Nurturing styles, social impacts, and educational encounters can shape how disposition shows and develops into more perplexing character attributes. A strong and supporting climate might improve positive characteristics, while unfriendly encounters or disregard can add to the advancement of maladaptive character designs.

4. **Estimation of Demeanor and Character Attributes**

4.1. Psychometric Instruments

Different psychometric apparatuses have been created to survey both demeanor and character attributes. These instruments are intended to give a quantitative and normalized proportion of a singular's qualities. For demeanor, instruments like the Baby Conduct Poll (IBQ) and the Youngsters' Conduct Survey (CBQ) are generally utilized. In the domain of character, appraisals, for example, the Modified NEO Character Stock (NEO-PI-R) and the Enormous Five Stock (BFI) are broadly utilized.

4.2. Social Perceptions

Observational strategies assume a vital part in figuring out personality, particularly in youth. Scientists and clinicians might notice babies and youngsters in different settings to survey their responses to novel improvements, level of movement, and social collaborations. These perceptions give significant experiences into the youngster's disposition and can illuminate forecasts about future character improvement.

4.3. Self-Reports and Meetings

Self-report measures include people giving data about their own demeanor and character through polls or meetings. While these strategies are advantageous and broadly utilized, they are liable to predispositions like social attractiveness. Notwithstanding, self-reports can offer significant emotional experiences into a singular's self-discernment and familiarity with their own attributes.

5. **The Job of Demeanor and Character in Regular day to day existence**

5.1. Connections and Social Communications

Disposition and character qualities essentially impact how people explore social cooperations and structure connections. For example, people with elevated degrees of extraversion might be more skilled at starting and keeping up with social associations, while those with elevated degrees of pleasantness might add to positive and amicable connections.

5.2. Vocation Decisions and Achievement

Character qualities assume a part in vocation decisions and expert achievement. Honest people are much of the time pursued in work settings because of their unwavering quality and tirelessness. Imaginative and open people might flourish in callings that require development, while those with a serious level of neuroticism might succeed in jobs that request close to home responsiveness and sympathy.

5.3. Psychological wellness Suggestions

Certain character attributes and volatile inclinations are related with emotional well-being results. For example, elevated degrees of neuroticism are connected to an expanded gamble of tension and discouragement. Understanding these affiliations can be critical in the anticipation, finding, and treatment of psychological wellness issues.

6. Difficulties and Discussions in Exploration

6.1. Nature versus Sustain Discussion

The well established discussion of nature versus support stays applicable in the investigation of demeanor and character. While disposition is considered to have areas of strength for a premise, the impact of natural variables can't be disregarded. The unpredictable transaction among hereditary qualities and climate presents moves in secluding explicit commitments to demeanor and character advancement.

6.2. Social Varieties

The comprehensiveness of specific character qualities and unstable aspects is a subject of progressing research. Social varieties in values, standards, and assumptions might affect the articulation and translation of characteristics. Analysts should explore the test of growing socially touchy evaluations that catch the subtleties of demeanor and character across assorted populaces.

6.3. Dynamic Nature of Character

Character isn't static however unique, with qualities possibly advancing over the life expectancy. The steadiness of specific attributes and the flexibility of others present difficulties in anticipating long haul results in view of early personality appraisals. Longitudinal examinations are fundamental for following the direction of character advancement and understanding the variables that add to strength or change.

2. Basic Obedience Skills

Essential submission abilities are basic to cultivating a positive and helpful connection among canines and their proprietors. These abilities not just add to a polite canine buddy yet additionally upgrade the general personal satisfaction for both the canine and its human family. In this exhaustive aide, we will investigate the significance of fundamental dutifulness, the key abilities included, and compelling preparation strategies to guarantee an agreeable connection among canines and their proprietors.

1. The Meaning of Essential Submission

1.1. Building Correspondence

Fundamental dutifulness abilities act as a typical language among canines and their proprietors. At the point when a canine gets it and answers fundamental orders, it works with correspondence and encourages a feeling of shared understanding. This correspondence is fundamental for conveying assumptions, guaranteeing wellbeing, and reinforcing the connection between the canine and its proprietor.

1.2. Guaranteeing Wellbeing

Essential compliance is pivotal for the security of both the canine and individuals around it. Orders, for example, "sit," "remain," and "come" can forestall possibly perilous circumstances, for example, a canine running into traffic or moving toward new or forceful canines. These abilities are particularly significant in broad daylight spaces and can be life-saving in crisis circumstances.

1.3. Improving Socialization

Respectful canines are bound to be invited in different group environments. Essential acquiescence abilities empower canines to connect emphatically with individuals, different creatures, and the climate. A socially skilled canine isn't just a delight to be near yet additionally encounters less pressure and uneasiness in various circumstances.

2. Key Fundamental Dutifulness Abilities

2.1. Sit

"Sit" is quite possibly of the most major and broadly involved order in canine preparation. Training a canine to sit on order helps in overseeing conduct as well as makes way for different orders. A flexible expertise can be applied in different circumstances, like hello visitors, holding up at entryways, or getting ready for different orders.

Preparing Tip: Begin with a treat close by and hold it over the canine's head, moving it somewhat in reverse. As the canine lifts its head to follow the treat, its rump will normally bring down into a sitting position. Promptly reward the way of behaving with the treat and uplifting feedback.

2.2. Remain

The "remain" order is fundamental for keeping a canine in a particular situation until given further guidance. This expertise is especially helpful in circumstances where a canine requirements to stay in one spot, for example, during prepping, when outsiders approach, or while going across the road.

Preparing Tip: Start with the canine in a sitting position. Open your hand, palm confronting the canine, and say "remain" while making a stride back. On the off chance that the canine remaining parts set up, award and commendation. Progressively increment the term and distance as the canine turns out to be more OK with the order.

2.3. Come

"Come" is an imperative order for review, guaranteeing that a canine revisitations of its proprietor immediately when called. This order isn't just helpful for wellbeing yet additionally cultivates a feeling of trust and dependability between the canine and its proprietor.

Preparing Tip: Utilize a rope at first to tenderly guide the canine toward you as you say "come." When the canine contacts you, prize and commendation. Bit by bit increment the distance and practice in various conditions to support the order in different settings.

2.4. Down

The "down" order educates the canine to rests and is useful for overseeing edgy way of behaving, forestalling bouncing, and advancing serenity.

Preparing Tip: Begin with the canine in a sitting position. Grasp a treat and lower it to the ground before the canine, saying "down." As the canine follows the treat, guide it into a lying position. Award and acclaim when the canine effectively rests.

2.5. Leave It

"Leave it" is an order intended to keep a canine from drawing closer, getting, or communicating with unfortunate articles or substances. This ability is fundamental for the security of the canine and can be applied in circumstances where the canine experiences possibly unsafe things.

Preparing Tip: Spot a treat in your shut hand and present it to the canine without allowing it to get to the treat. At the point when the canine quits attempting to move the treat and steps back, say "leave it" and compensation with an alternate treat. Slowly increment the trouble by utilizing additional enticing things.

3. **Compelling Preparation Strategies**

3.1. Uplifting feedback

Uplifting feedback includes compensating wanted ways of behaving to energize their reiteration. Whether utilizing treats, recognition, or play, uplifting feedback fortifies the association between the order and the way of behaving. Canines learn all the more really when they partner orders with positive results.

Tip: Utilize high-esteem treats to propel and compensate the canine at first. Progressively change to irregular awards as the way of behaving turns out to be more reliable.

3.2. Consistency

Consistency is key in canine preparation. Everybody in the family ought to utilize similar orders and procedures to stay away from disarray. Build up appropriate conduct reliably and try not to accidentally compensate undesired ways of behaving.

Tip: Make a rundown of orders and guarantee that all relatives are know about and utilize a similar wording. Consistency in assumptions and prizes will add to a thoroughly prepared canine.

3.3. Tolerance and Timing

Preparing takes time, and tolerance is an uprightness while working with canines. Show restraint, particularly with young doggies or canines mastering new abilities. Moreover, timing is vital; reward the ideal way of behaving quickly to fortify the relationship between the order and the activity.

Tip: Be aware of your timing while conveying treats or commendation. The nearer the prize is to the ideal way of behaving, the more successful it will be in building up that way of behaving.

3.4. Slow Movement

Preparing ought to advance slowly to guarantee that the canine expands on its abilities at an agreeable speed. Start with basic orders and gradually increment intricacy as the canine turns out to be more capable. This approach forestalls disappointment and keeps the preparation experience positive.

Tip: Expert one order prior to presenting another one. As the canine turns out to be more sure and reliable, steadily add interruptions or practice in various conditions to build up the orders in different settings.

4. Investigating Normal Difficulties

4.1. Absence of Inspiration

On the off chance that a canine seems uninterested or unmotivated during preparing, it very well might be useful to reconsider the prizes being utilized. Explore different avenues regarding various treats or toys to recognize what spurs the canine. Furthermore, guarantee that instructional courses are kept short and pleasant to keep up with the canine's advantage.

4.2. Interruptions

Canines can undoubtedly become diverted, particularly in new or animating conditions. While preparing in various settings, begin with recognizable orders and bit by bit present interruptions. Increment the trouble steadily, compensating the canine for keeping up with center in the midst of interruptions.

4.3. Irregularity in Orders

Irregularity in orders can befuddle a canine and impede the educational experience. Guarantee that everybody engaged with the canine's preparation utilizes similar orders and procedures. Consistency in language and assumptions will add to an all the more respectful canine.

B. Preparing Your Cat for Certification

Confirming your feline may not be pretty much as normal as canine preparation, yet it tends to be a remunerating try that upgrades the connection among you and your catlike companion. While felines are known for their free nature, they can learn different ways of behaving and deceives through uplifting feedback. Here is a manual for assist you with setting up your feline for certificate.

Pick the Right Certificate Program:

Research and pick a certificate program that lines up with your feline's capacities and your preparation objectives. Search for programs that emphasis on encouraging feedback strategies and perceive various abilities and ways of behaving.

Begin with Fundamental Orders:

Start with fundamental orders, for example, "sit," "remain," and "come." Use treats or toys as remunerations to persuade your feline. Continue to prepare meetings short and positive to keep up with your feline's advantage and excitement.

Progressive Presentations:

Present new orders and ways of behaving slowly. Felines might find opportunity to change, so be patient and celebrate little triumphs. Consistency is critical, so utilize similar signs and rewards each time.

Encouraging feedback:

Encouraging feedback is essential for feline preparation. Reward your feline promptly when they play out the ideal way of behaving. This makes positive affiliations and energizes redundancy.

Clicker Preparing:

Consider utilizing a clicker as a preparation help. Clicker preparing includes partner a clicker with a prize. This reasonable correspondence assists your feline with understanding when they've played out the ideal way of behaving.

Desensitize to Taking care of:

Numerous confirmation projects might require your feline to endure taking care of. Slowly desensitize your feline to being contacted, prepped, or inspected. Reward them for quiet way of behaving during these cooperations.

Practice in Various Conditions:

Train your feline in different conditions to sum up their abilities. This guarantees that they can perform orders in various circumstances, which might be a prerequisite for confirmation.

Sealing Ways of behaving:

Sealing includes building up ways of behaving within the sight of interruptions. Slowly acquaint interruptions during preparing with guarantee your feline can keep up with center and perform orders in true circumstances.

Look for Proficient Direction:

Think about looking for direction from proficient feline coaches or behaviorists. They can give customized counsel, distinguish explicit difficulties, and assist you with fitting your preparation approach.

Partake All the while:

Preparing ought to be a pleasant encounter for both you and your feline. Keep meetings positive, and on the off chance that your feline appears to be uninterested or pushed, have some time off and attempt once more at a later time.

By following these means and staying patient and predictable, you can set up your feline for confirmation effectively. The cycle not just gives mental feeling to your catlike friend yet in addition fortifies the extraordinary bond you share. Recall that each feline is an individual, so tailor your preparation way to deal with suit your feline's character and inclinations.

Chapter 2

Basic Commands For Therapy Cats

The job of treatment felines in offering profound help, solace, and friendship to people in need has earned far reaching respect. To guarantee treatment felines can successfully satisfy their jobs, it is vital for train them in fundamental orders that work with positive communications and guarantee a protected and controlled climate. This extensive aide will investigate the significance of essential orders for treatment felines, the preparation cycle, and how these orders add to fruitful treatment work.

1. The Job of Treatment Felines

1.1. Significance of Essential Orders

Essential orders are the groundwork of a treatment feline's preparation. They improve the feline's way of behaving as well as empower overseers to oversee and direct their catlike buddies during treatment meetings. Thoroughly prepared treatment felines add to a positive and unsurprising climate, which is urgent for people looking for daily reassurance or friendship.

1.2. Advantages of Treatment Feline Preparation

1. **Security**

   Preparing treatment felines in fundamental orders guarantees their wellbeing and the security of those they associate with. Orders like "remain" and "leave it" are especially important in forestalling undesirable ways of behaving.

2. **Solace**

   A treatment feline's capacity to answer orders establishes an agreeable and controlled climate for people managing pressure, nervousness, or other inner difficulties.

3. **Positive Cooperations**

Fundamental orders empower treatment felines to participate in sure associations, upgrading their adequacy in giving solace and basic encouragement.

II. Essential Orders for Treatment Felines

2.1. Sit

The "sit" order is central for treatment felines. Helping a feline to sit on order gives a controlled and harmless stance, making communications more receptive for those looking for solace.

Preparing Tip: Use treats or toys as uplifting feedback. Tenderly press down on the feline's lower back while saying "sit." Award the feline when it sits, partner the activity with the order.

2.2. Remain

"Remain" is a urgent order for treatment felines, guaranteeing they stay in an assigned region or with a person on a case by case basis. This order improves security and control during treatment meetings.

Preparing Tip: Begin with brief lengths and bit by bit increment the time. Use treats and applause to remunerate the feline for remaining set up.

2.3. Come

The "come" order is fundamental for treatment felines to move toward people or return to their overseers when required. This order improves the feline's responsiveness and supports a feeling of association.

Preparing Tip: Urge the feline to drop by utilizing a well disposed tone and offering treats. Slowly increment the distance and practice in different conditions.

2.4. Leave It

"Leave it" is an important order for treatment felines to try not to connect with articles or substances that might be available during meetings. This order guarantees a protected and controlled climate.

Preparing Tip: Utilize a treat or toy to occupy the feline from the objective item and say "leave it." Prize the feline for moving its concentrate away from the thing.

2.5. Delicate Touch

Showing a treatment feline to utilize a delicate touch is gainful for cooperations where actual contact is involved. This order forestalls unexpected scratching or harsh play.

Preparing Tip: Urge the feline to involve a delicate touch by offering your hand for it to nestle or contact with its paw. Reward delicate communications with treats and applause.

2.6. Down

The "down" order educates the feline to rests, advancing a cool headed disposition during treatment meetings. This order is especially helpful while cooperating with people who might favor a situated or lying feline.

Preparing Tip: Use gets and delicate direction urge the feline to rests. Reward the way of behaving and partner it with the "down" order.

2.7. No

While uplifting feedback is an essential preparation approach, showing a treatment feline the "no" order can be valuable in diverting unwanted ways of behaving. This order ought to be utilized sparingly and with a delicate tone.

Preparing Tip: Say "no" immovably and promptly divert the feline to a proper way of behaving. Reward the feline when it agrees with the redirection.

III. Preparing Strategies for Treatment Felines

3.1. Encouraging feedback

Uplifting feedback is the best and others conscious preparation strategy for treatment felines. Compensating wanted ways of behaving with treats, recognition, or play builds up those ways of behaving, making the feline bound to rehash them.

Tip: Utilize high-esteem treats to persuade the feline during instructional meetings. Consistency in remunerations assists the feline with partner positive results with explicit orders.

3.2. Clicker Preparing

Clicker preparing is an exact and clear method for speaking with treatment felines. By partner a clicker with a prize, overseers can check the specific second the feline shows the ideal way of behaving.

Tip: Snap following the feline plays out the ideal way of behaving, trailed by a treat. This unmistakable correspondence helps with quicker learning and support.

3.3. Short and Positive Meetings

Continue to prepare meetings short and positive to keep up with the feline's advantage and forestall weakness or stress. Felines stand out ranges, so short, it are more powerful to connect with meetings.

Tip: Go for the gold moment meetings and finish strong, regardless of whether it implies achieving only one order.

3.4. Steady Movement

Present orders steadily, beginning with the rudiments and advancing to further developed abilities. Expand on the feline's triumphs to continue instructional meetings pleasant and testing.

Tip: Expert one order prior to presenting another one. This bit by bit approach guarantees a strong groundwork and forestalls overpower.

3.5. Persistence and Consistency

Persistence is pivotal while preparing treatment felines. Felines might find opportunity to comprehend and answer orders, so stay patient and predictable in your preparation endeavors.

Tip: Be steady with orders, prizes, and assumptions. Felines blossom with routine and consistency, which upholds successful learning.

3.6. Preparing in Different Conditions

Open treatment felines to various conditions to sum up their abilities. Rehearsing orders in different settings assists the feline with adjusting to new circumstances and stay responsive during treatment meetings.

Tip: Bit by bit present interruptions and practice orders in various rooms or open air spaces to build up the feline's capacity to answer in different conditions.

IV. Certificate Cycle for Treatment Felines

4.1. Picking a Confirmation Program

While guaranteeing a treatment feline, pick a respectable certificate program that lines up with your objectives and values. Search for programs that stress encouraging feedback and survey various abilities applicable to treatment work.

4.2. Essential Assessment Rules

Confirmation programs ordinarily survey a treatment feline's fundamental personality, compliance, and conduct during recreated treatment meetings. The feline ought to exhibit a quiet disposition, responsiveness to orders, and suitable connections with people.

4.3. Planning for Affirmation

Set up your treatment feline for accreditation by deliberately investigating and rehearsing essential orders. Guarantee the feline is OK with different taking care of situations and stays centered during mimicked treatment collaborations.

4.4. Reproduced Treatment Meetings

During certificate, the feline might be assessed in mimicked treatment situations. This can incorporate associations with people of differing ages, reactions to startling upgrades, and adherence to fundamental orders.

4.5. Kept Preparing and Schooling

Confirmation is definitely not a one-time accomplishment; continuous preparation and training are fundamental for keeping a treatment feline's abilities. Remain informed about new preparation strategies and keep on supporting essential orders all through the feline's treatment profession.

V. Defeating Difficulties in Preparing

5.1. Individual Contrasts

Perceive that each feline is special, and preparing approaches might should be custom-made to suit individual contrasts in demeanor, inspiration, and learning style.

5.2. Dread or Uneasiness

On the off chance that a treatment feline displays dread or tension during preparing, recognize and address the hidden causes. Dial back the preparation pace, make a positive relationship with instructional courses, and give a protected climate.

5.3. Interruptions

Felines can be quickly drawn offtrack, particularly in new conditions. Steadily present interruptions during preparing, guaranteeing the feline remaining parts responsive even in animating or new settings.

1. Calm and Gentle Interactions

Quiet and delicate communications structure the foundation of positive connections, cultivating associations that are both significant and enhancing.

Whether in private connections, proficient settings, or cooperations with creatures, the characteristics of serenity and tenderness add to an amicable and sustaining climate. In this investigation, we dig into the meaning of quiet and delicate collaborations, their effect on different parts of life, and procedures to develop and upgrade these characteristics for additional satisfying associations.

1. Grasping Serenity and Delicacy

1.1. Serenity

Serenity is a condition of peacefulness, where one's feelings and responses are estimated and consistent. It includes the capacity to stay under control notwithstanding difficulties, explore stressors without elevated reactivity, and make a climate of soundness.

1.2. Tenderness

Delicacy, then again, mirrors an obliging and delicate methodology in communications. It includes being gentle in personality, staying away from cruelty, and treating others with graciousness and compassion. Tenderness envelops actual activities, verbally expressed words, and generally speaking attitude.

2. The Significance of Quiet and Delicate Collaborations

2.1. Building Trust

Quiet and delicate connections fabricate trust by establishing a free from any potential harm climate. At the point when people feel that they are treated with deference and generosity, trust thrives, shaping the underpinning areas of strength for of tough connections.

2.2. Improving Correspondence

Tranquility and delicacy improve correspondence by encouraging transparency and receptivity. In a quiet and delicate air, people are bound to communicate their thoughts truly, prompting better getting it and association.

2.3. Relieving Struggle

The capacity to keep quiet and delicate is an incredible asset in relieving struggle. Rather than heightening pressures, people who approach clashes with a quiet and delicate disposition can work with goal and keep up with the trustworthiness of connections.

2.4. Advancing Close to home Prosperity

Quiet and delicate communications add to profound prosperity by establishing a positive and steady close to home environment. Such cooperations lessen pressure, tension, and cynicism, advancing a feeling that everything is good and profound equilibrium.

3. Quiet and Delicate Associations in Various Settings

3.1. Individual Connections

1. **Heartfelt Associations**

   In close connections, quiet and delicate cooperations are fundamental for keeping up with closeness and congruity. Communicating affection, appreciation, and understanding in a delicate way fortifies the profound connection between accomplices.

2. **Relational peculiarities**

Inside families, quiet and delicate connections add to a sustaining climate. Guardians who approach their youngsters with tenderness and serenity give a protected establishment to profound and mental development.

3.2. Proficient Settings

1. **Work environment Connections**

   In the work environment, quiet and delicate cooperations cultivate a positive corporate culture. Pioneers who display these characteristics establish a workplace where representatives feel esteemed, heard, and propelled.

2. **Client and Client Relations**

In business communications, smoothness and tenderness add to successful client and client relations. Building trust and offering magnificent support are improved when these characteristics are focused on.

3.3. Cooperations with Creatures

Quiet and delicate cooperations with creatures are urgent for their prosperity. Whether as pet people, overseers, or experts working with creatures, moving toward them with delicacy and tranquility constructs trust and guarantees their physical and close to home wellbeing.

IV. Systems for Developing Quiet and Delicate Associations

4.1. Care Practices

1. **Reflection**

   Care reflection develops a quiet and focused mentality. By routinely captivating in reflection rehearses, people can upgrade their capacity to stay made and delicate in different circumstances.
2. **Profound Relaxing**

Profound breathing activities are viable for quieting the sensory system. Integrating cognizant breathing into everyday schedules assists people with keeping a feeling of serenity and answer nicely in communications.

4.2. The capacity to appreciate people on a deeper level Turn of events

1. **Mindfulness**

   Understanding one's own feelings is essential for developing quiet and delicate communications. Creating mindfulness permits people to successfully deal with their close to home reactions more.
2. **Sympathy**

Compassion is the way to delicacy in connections. By getting it and discussing the thoughts of others, people can answer with benevolence and thought, making a positive and steady climate.

4.3. Relational abilities

1. **Undivided attention**

   Undivided attention is a basic correspondence expertise that adds to tenderness. Giving full focus and genuinely hearing what others are talking about encourages understanding and compassion.
2. **Peaceful Correspondence**

The standards of peaceful correspondence underscore communicating requirements and sentiments without judgment. This approach advances delicate associations by trying not to fault and encourage valuable discourse.

4.4. Stress The board Procedures

1. **Using time productively**

   Compelling using time productively decreases pressure and permits people to move toward collaborations with a more loosened up mentality.

   By staying away from surged discussions, individuals can take part in more settled and more significant collaborations.

2. **Solid Way of life Decisions**

Standard activity, a reasonable eating routine, and adequate rest add to in general prosperity. These way of life decisions emphatically influence a singular's capacity to stay cool and delicate in different circumstances.

4.5. Compromise Abilities

1. **Critical thinking**

   Moving toward clashes with a critical thinking outlook adds to quiet and valuable goals. Recognizing shared objectives and looking for commonly valuable arrangements improves the nature of cooperations.

2. **Profound Guideline**

Figuring out how to direct feelings is urgent for keeping up with serenity in struggle circumstances. Procedures, for example, care and mental rebuilding assist people with dealing with their close to home reactions actually.

V. Challenges in Carrying out Quiet and Delicate Connections

5.1. Individual Stressors

People might battle with carrying out quiet and delicate connections when confronted with individual stressors. Perceiving and tending to these stressors is fundamental for keeping a positive methodology in connections.

5.2. Social Contrasts

Social standards and correspondence styles fluctuate, and what might be viewed as quiet and delicate in one culture might vary in another. Monitoring and conscious toward social contrasts is essential for effective communications.

5.3. Profound Triggers

Close to home triggers can think twice about's capacity to keep quiet and delicate. Distinguishing and understanding these triggers permits people to foster techniques for dealing with profound reactions.

VI. Showing Quiet and Delicate Cooperations to Youngsters

6.1. Job Displaying

Youngsters advance by noticing the way of behaving of grown-ups around them. Guardians, parental figures, and teachers can display quiet and delicate cooperations in their day to day routines, giving an outline to youngsters to follow.

6.2. Profound Proficiency Schooling

Showing youngsters about feelings and how to communicate them properly is fundamental for cultivating quiet and delicate collaborations. Close to home education programs in schools add to the advancement of compassionate and chivalrous people.

6.3. Compromise Abilities

Engaging kids with compromise abilities assists them with exploring social cooperations all the more really. Training them to communicate their necessities and sentiments serenely adds to positive connections.

1. **Teaching Gentle Petting**

   Showing delicate petting is a pivotal part of cultivating positive connections among people and creatures. Whether connecting with canines, felines, or different pets, the manner in which people handle and contact creatures fundamentally influences the general insight for the two players. In this thorough aide, we will investigate the significance of delicate petting, the advantages it brings to human-creature connections, and down to earth methodologies for educating and advancing this delicate methodology.

   The Meaning of Delicate Petting

   Laying out Trust and Solace

   Delicate petting is a fundamental component in building trust among people and creatures. At the point when pets experience delicate, harmless touch, they are bound to have a solid sense of reassurance and agreeable in their communications. This trust shapes the premise of a positive and secure relationship.

   Profound Prosperity of the Pet

   The profound prosperity of pets is straightforwardly impacted by how they are contacted and petted. Delicate petting adds to a feeling that everything is good, lessens pressure and uneasiness, and improves the generally profound strength of the creature. Understanding and regarding a creature's limits through delicate petting is fundamental for their joy.

   Uplifting feedback for Wanted Conduct

   Delicate petting fills in as a type of uplifting feedback for pets. At the point when creatures are petted delicately, it supports positive way of behaving, empowering them to look for and appreciate human communication. This positive affiliation elevates an eagerness to draw in and collaborate in different exercises.

   Forestalling Dread and Hostility

   Harsh or improper dealing with can prompt apprehension and animosity in pets. Showing delicate petting forestalls these negative responses by guaranteeing that the creature feels good and secure during human contact. This is especially significant in forestalling dread based conduct issues.

   Showing Delicate Petting to Youngsters

   Managed Cooperation

   Managed cooperation among youngsters and pets is fundamental while showing delicate petting. Grown-ups ought to show and guide youngsters on the most proficient method to approach and contact creatures delicately. This not just guarantees the security of both the kid and the pet yet in addition lays out early illustrations in sympathy and empathy.

Exhibiting Appropriate Procedure

Guardians and parental figures assume a crucial part in showing the legitimate procedure for delicate petting. This includes utilizing slow and delicate strokes, staying away from unexpected developments, and regarding the pet's non-verbal communication. Youngsters advance by perception, and positive job demonstrating makes way for aware and agreeable connections.

Showing Appreciation for Limits

Instructing youngsters about regarding the limits of creatures is pivotal. Understanding that pets may not necessarily need to be contacted or may have explicit regions they are delicate about assists youngsters with creating compassion and thought. Training them to notice the pet's signs for solace or inconvenience is fundamental.

Techniques for Showing Delicate Petting

Figuring out Pet Non-verbal communication

A key part of showing delicate petting is grasping pet non-verbal communication. Perceiving indications of solace, for example, murmuring or swaying tails, and indications of distress, as smoothed ears or snarling, permits people to appropriately change their methodology. This mindfulness is imperative in making positive and peaceful cooperations.

Continuous Prologue to Contact

For pets, particularly those not familiar with human touch, a steady presentation is critical. Begin with short meetings of delicate petting and continuously increment the term as the pet turns out to be more agreeable. This approach is especially significant for salvage creatures or those with a background marked by injury.

Encouraging feedback

Encouraging feedback is an incredible asset in training pets to appreciate delicate petting. Consolidate delicate strokes with treats, recognition, or most loved toys to make a positive affiliation. This supports that delicate petting prompts positive results, empowering the pet to look for and appreciate human touch.

Consistency in Approach

Consistency is pivotal in showing delicate petting. Whether it's a family with different individuals or a gathering of companions cooperating with a similar pet, everybody ought to embrace a predictable methodology. This guarantees that the pet gets a brought together message about what comprises delicate and OK touch.

Utilizing Delicate and Sluggish Developments

The actual methodology matters while showing delicate petting. Utilize delicate and sluggish developments to try not to surprise the pet. Fast or sudden signals can set off dread or tension. By keeping a quiet and purposeful touch, people establish a climate wherein pets can unwind and partake in the collaboration.

Giving Places of refuge

Pets ought to continuously approach places of refuge where they can withdraw on the off chance that they feel overpowered. Helping people to perceive when a pet necessities space and permitting them to separate from connection advances a feeling of independence for the pet. This shows regard for the creature's limits and solace levels.

Grasping Different Pet Inclinations

Varieties Among Species

Various species have fluctuating inclinations with regards to petting. Canines might appreciate gut rubs, while felines might incline toward delicate strokes along their back. Understanding these species-explicit inclinations is essential in guaranteeing that the petting experience is charming for the creature.

Individual Pet Inclinations

Inside an animal groups, individual pets might have one of a kind inclinations. A few creatures might appreciate being petted on unambiguous regions, while others might be more delicate. Noticing and regarding these singular inclinations add to a custom fitted and positive collaboration for each pet.

Tending to Difficulties in Showing Delicate Petting

Unfortunate or Damaged Pets

Unfortunate or damaged pets might require additional persistence and delicate prologue to contact. Gradually assembling trust, utilizing uplifting feedback, and permitting the pet to start contact can assist conquer dread and make positive relationship with delicate petting.

Overexcitement or Energy

A few pets might become overexcited or energetic during communications. While excitement is positive, it's pivotal to help people to perceive when a pet requirements a break. Excessively unpleasant play ought to be deterred, and delicate petting can be once again introduced after a short delay.

Wellbeing related Awarenesses

Pets with medical problems might have explicit awarenesses or regions that ought to be stayed away from during petting. Helping people to know about potential wellbeing related concerns guarantees that the pet's prosperity is focused on. Talking with a veterinarian can give direction on suitable taking care of to pets with explicit medical issue.

2. **Encouraging Relaxed Behavior**

Empowering loosened up conduct in different settings, whether with pets, in private connections, or inside oneself, is a strong practice that adds to by and large prosperity. Developing a feeling of tranquility and solace encourages a good climate, lessens pressure, and upgrades the nature of connections. In this investigation, we will dig into the significance of empowering loosened up conduct, its advantages, and useful systems to advance a more serene and amicable environment.

The Meaning of Empowering Loosened up Conduct

1. **Stress Decrease**

   Empowering loosened up conduct is a critical part in pressure decrease. In the present high speed world, stress is common, influencing mental and actual wellbeing. By establishing a climate that cultivates unwinding, people can check the pessimistic impacts of pressure and advance in general prosperity.

2. **Upgraded Connections**

   In private connections, empowering loosened up conduct fortifies associations. At the point when people feel quiet and agreeable, correspondence improves, and connections extend.

   This is material not exclusively to human cooperations yet in addition to associations with pets, where a casual climate adds to trust and positive commitment.

3. **Further developed Concentration and Efficiency**

   A casual brain is more engaged and useful. In work or scholastic settings, people who can keep a feeling of tranquility are better prepared to deal with difficulties, tackle issues, and use wise judgment. Empowering a casual setting in these settings can prompt expanded proficiency and imagination.

4. **Physical and Psychological wellness Advantages**

Loosened up conduct is related with various medical advantages. Physiologically, it can prompt lower pulse, worked on insusceptible capability, and better rest. Mentally, a casual state adds to a positive outlook, decreased uneasiness, and upgraded profound prosperity.

Down to earth Systems for Empowering Loosened up Conduct

1. **Care Practices**
1. **Reflection:**

   Empowering people to participate in care contemplation is a strong technique. Reflection develops a present-centered mindfulness, assisting people with relinquishing stressors and embrace a more loosened up state. Basic directed reflection meetings or the act of care breathing can be successful devices.

2. Profound Relaxing:

Profound breathing activities are effectively available and can be drilled anyplace. Training people to take slow, full breaths enacts the body's unwinding reaction, diminishing pressure and advancing a feeling of smoothness.

2. Establishing Agreeable Conditions

1. **Actual Solace:**
   Guaranteeing actual solace adds to loosened up conduct. Open to seating, comfortable spaces, and fitting lighting all assume a part in establishing a climate where people feel quiet.
2. **Temperature Guideline:**

Keeping an ideal temperature in indoor spaces is urgent. Being too hot or too cold can be diverting and add to pressure. Guaranteeing an agreeable temperature cultivates a casual air.

3. Empowering Open Correspondence

Open correspondence is essential in private connections. Empowering people to offer their viewpoints and sentiments without judgment advances understanding and diminishes strain. This open trade adds to an in general loose and positive relationship dynamic.

4. Laying out Normal Breaks

In work or scholarly settings, normal breaks are fundamental for forestalling burnout and empowering unwinding. Brief breaks during the day permit people to re-energize, pull together, and move toward undertakings with a more loosened up outlook.

5. Advancing Actual Prosperity

1. **Normal Activity:**
   Active work is a characteristic pressure reliever. Empowering customary activity, whether through strolling, running, yoga, or different exercises, adds to in general prosperity and keeps a casual state.
2. **Solid Sustenance:**

Diet assumes a critical part in physical and psychological well-being. A reasonable and nutritious eating regimen upholds in general prosperity, adding to a loose and stimulated state.

6. Careful Pet Connections

For those with pets, connections with creatures can be a wellspring of unwinding. Empowering delicate petting, establishing a quiet climate for pets, and investing quality energy with them add to a feeling of tranquility for both the pet and the proprietor.

7. Setting Practical Assumptions

Empowering loosened up conduct includes setting practical assumptions. Unreasonable requests or objectives can prompt pressure and strain. Assisting people with setting reachable targets advances a more loosened up way to deal with life's difficulties.

Challenges in Empowering Loosened up Conduct

1. **Social and Cultural Tensions**

   Social and cultural tensions can make assumptions that focus on efficiency over prosperity. Empowering loosened up conduct might confront obstruction in conditions where stress and hecticness are seen as marks of accomplishment.

2. **Individual Contrasts**

   Individual contrasts in character and strategies for dealing with stress can introduce difficulties. What might be unwinding for one individual may not be for another. Fitting procedures to individual inclinations and necessities is fundamental.

3. **Working environment Assumptions**

Working environment societies that focus on consistent efficiency might find it trying to embrace a casual methodology. Moving hierarchical perspectives and advancing a solid balance between serious and fun activities are continuous difficulties.

Empowering Loosened up Conduct in Kids

1. **Making Quiet Schedules**

   Laying out quiet and unsurprising schedules adds to loosened up conduct in kids. Steady sleep time customs, supper time schedules, and assigned unwinding periods give a feeling that all is well with the world.

2. **Showing Unwinding Procedures**

   Basic unwinding methods customized for youngsters, like profound breathing or directed symbolism, can be presented. These strategies enable youngsters to oversee pressure and feelings in a sound manner.

3. **Adjusting Exercises**

Empowering a harmony between scholarly, extracurricular, and relaxation exercises is pivotal. Over booking can prompt pressure, while a balanced methodology advances unwinding and by and large prosperity.

B. Sit and Stay Commands for Therapy Visits

The "Sit" and "Remain" orders are key devices in planning treatment creatures for effective and positive visits. These orders give an establishment to respectful connections, guaranteeing a controlled and agreeable climate for both the treatment creature and the people they are there to help.

The "Sit" order trains the treatment creature to expect a situated situation on sign. This not just presents a quiet and harmless stance, making the creature more congenial, however it likewise deals with the degree of fervor during treatment visits. People, particularly the individuals who might be worried or restless, find a sitting treatment creature less scary, working with smoother presentations and communications.

Similarly significant is the "Remain" order, which trains the treatment creature to stay in an assigned position. Whether sitting or resting, the capacity to remain set up is significant for keeping up with control and guaranteeing an engaged and mindful presence during treatment meetings.

This order permits the overseer to direct the treatment creature through different situations without superfluous development, establishing a steady and secure climate for all interested parties.

In treatment visits, these orders add to the consistency and construction of associations. At the point when people realize they can move toward a treatment creature that is tranquilly situated or remaining set up, it lays out a feeling of safety and energizes commitment. In addition, these orders empower controllers to deal with the speed and stream of the treatment meeting, guaranteeing that the creature's way of behaving lines up with the particular necessities and solace levels of those getting treatment.

Chapter 3

Building Confidence In Unfamiliar Environments

Building trust in new conditions is an essential expertise that enables people to explore new circumstances with strength and balance. Whether in private, expert, or scholastic settings, the capacity to adjust and flourish in new environmental elements is vital to self-awareness and achievement. This far reaching guide investigates the significance of certainty, the elements impacting it, and viable procedures for building and keeping up with trust in different new conditions.

1. **Grasping Certainty**

   1.1. Meaning of Certainty

   Certainty is a diverse mental state described by confidence, faith in one's capacities, and an uplifting perspective. A fundamental quality impacts how people approach difficulties, simply decide, and interface with others.

   1.2. Significance of Certainty

   Certainty is an impetus for self-awareness and achievement. It influences different parts of life, including professional success, scholastic accomplishment, relationship building, and generally prosperity. People who radiate certainty are bound to face challenges, embrace open doors, and successfully defeat hindrances.

2. **Factors Affecting Certainty**

   2.1. Previous Encounters

   Positive previous encounters add to certainty, supporting the conviction that one can explore new conditions effectively. On the other hand, negative encounters might dissolve certainty, requiring deliberate endeavors to remake confidence.

   2.2. Self-Adequacy

   Self-adequacy, or one's faith in their capacity to accomplish explicit objectives, essentially impacts certainty. Fortifying self-viability includes defining reasonable objectives, breaking them down into sensible advances, and celebrating gradual accomplishments.

2.3. Emotionally supportive networks

A powerful emotionally supportive network, including companions, family, tutors, and partners, assumes a crucial part in building certainty. Positive consolation, valuable criticism, and a feeling of having a place add to a singular's confidence in their capacities.

2.4. Outlook and Positive Reasoning

Developing a positive outlook and rehearsing positive reasoning are instrumental in building certainty. Perceiving and testing negative self-talk, reexamining difficulties as any open doors for development, and zeroing in on qualities add to a more certain viewpoint.

3. **Building Trust in New Conditions**

3.1. Readiness and Exploration

Exhaustive planning and examination are fundamental for trust in new conditions. Procuring information about the new setting, figuring out its elements, and really getting to know potential difficulties ingrain a feeling of preparation.

3.2. Objective Setting

Laying out clear and feasible objectives in new conditions gives a guide to progress. Break bigger targets into more modest, reasonable errands, considering a bit by bit approach that forms certainty with every achievement.

3.3. Perception Procedures

Perception procedures include intellectually practicing effective results in new conditions. This training assists people with making a positive and certain psychological picture, diminishing uneasiness and improving their confidence in their capacity to explore what is going on.

3.4. Steady Openness

Steady openness to new conditions is a successful system for building certainty. Gradually expanding openness permits people to adjust, foster commonality, and gain trust in their capacity to adjust.

3.5. Positive Confirmations

Positive insistences support certainty by advancing a positive mental self view. Insistences that underscore qualities, strength, and versatility can balance self-uncertainty and cultivate a more sure outlook.

3.6. Looking for Mentorship

Mentorship gives significant direction and backing in new conditions.

Associating with guides who have insight in comparative circumstances permits people to acquire bits of knowledge, gain from others' encounters, and get useful criticism.

3.7. Embracing Difficulties as Any open doors

Seeing difficulties as any open doors for development reexamines the view of new conditions. Embracing difficulties with a positive mentality cultivates strength, versatility, and at last, trust in exploring new circumstances.

3.8. Building Relational Abilities

Creating solid relational abilities adds to trust in new friendly conditions. Successful correspondence, undivided attention, and the capacity to associate with others upgrade one's feeling of skill and straightforwardness in friendly cooperations.

4. Conquering Normal Difficulties in Building Certainty

4.1. Anxiety toward Disappointment

The feeling of dread toward disappointment is a typical test that can upset certainty. Embracing a development outlook, rethinking disappointment as a learning a potential open door, and zeroing in on the cycle as opposed to exclusively on results can moderate this trepidation.

4.2. Correlation with Others

Contrasting oneself with others can subvert certainty. Perceiving individual qualities, celebrating special characteristics, and understanding that everybody's process is different assist with encouraging a solid identity worth.

4.3. An inability to embrace success

An inability to embrace success, portrayed by feeling undeserving of achievement, can dissolve certainty. Looking for help, recognizing accomplishments, and rethinking negative considerations are compelling procedures for beating an inability to embrace success.

4.4. Absence of Self-Empathy

An absence of self-sympathy can hinder certainty building endeavors. Rehearsing self-empathy includes treating oneself with benevolence, recognizing blemishes, and understanding that difficulties are a characteristic piece of the growing experience.

5. Building Trust in Unambiguous Conditions

5.1. Proficient Conditions

In proficient settings, building certainty includes leveling up abilities, looking for constant learning open doors, and effectively taking part in vocation improvement. Successful correspondence, emphaticness, and a proactive mentality add to proficient certainty.

5.2. Scholarly Conditions

Building trust in scholarly conditions requires powerful review methodologies, using time effectively, and looking for scholastic help when required. Dynamic cooperation in class, drawing in with course material, and defining reasonable scholarly objectives encourage a certain scholastic outlook.

5.3. Social Conditions

Exploring social conditions with certainty includes areas of strength for creating abilities, developing significant associations, and embracing social open doors. Effectively captivating in friendly exercises, rehearsing undivided attention, and moving toward new associations with transparency add to social certainty.

5.4. Self-improvement Conditions

In conditions zeroed in on self-improvement, building certainty requires a promise to personal growth, reflection, and objective setting. Embracing difficulties, looking for criticism, and focusing on taking care of oneself add to trust in self-improvement ventures.

6. Keeping up with and Supporting Certainty

6.1. Intelligent Practices

Customary self-reflection is fundamental for keeping up with certainty. Occasionally assessing achievements, difficulties, and regions for development permits people to adjust their systems and keep building certainty over the long haul.

6.2. Learned

A pledge to kept learning upholds supported certainty. Effectively looking for new information, remaining informed about industry drifts, and chasing after proficient advancement valuable open doors add to continuous trust in proficient conditions.

6.3. Taking care of oneself

Focusing on taking care of oneself is urgent for keeping up with by and large prosperity and supporting certainty. Adjusting work, rest, and recreation exercises, alongside consolidating exercises that give pleasure and unwinding, adds to a strong and sure mentality.

6.4. Building an Encouraging group of people

Keeping major areas of strength for an organization gives continuous consolation and insistence. Developing associations with coaches, companions, and companions who offer positive help and valuable criticism reinforces certainty during the two triumphs and difficulties.

1. Exposing Your Cat to Different Settings

Felines are known for their free and regional nature, yet presenting them to various settings is a significant practice that can improve their prosperity and flexibility. Whether you're presenting another climate at home, taking your feline on movements, or essentially looking to improve their regular routine, presenting your feline to different settings adds to mental excitement, socialization, and a more satisfied cat buddy. In this far reaching guide, we will investigate the significance of presenting felines to various settings, the advantages it offers, and down to earth systems for a positive and effective experience.

1. **Figuring out the Feline's Inclination**

   ### 1.1. Regional Senses

   Felines have solid regional senses, and they frequently feel most good in natural environmental elements. Acquainting them with new settings ought to be done bit by bit and with aversion to their regular tendencies.

   ### 1.2. Individual Varieties

   Each feline is one of a kind in its reaction to new conditions. A few felines might be more bold and versatile, while others might be more wary and held. Understanding your feline's singular personality is vital while presenting them to various settings.

2. **Significance of Presenting Your Feline to Various Settings**

   ### 2.1. Mental Excitement

   Acquainting felines with new conditions gives mental excitement, forestalling weariness and advancing mental wellbeing. Novel encounters draw in their interest and critical thinking abilities, adding to a more enhanced and satisfied life.

   ### 2.2. Socialization

   Presenting your feline to various settings works with socialization, assisting them with turning out to be more agreeable around individuals, different creatures, and shifted boosts. Mingled felines are for the most part more sure, strong, and less inclined to pressure in new circumstances.

   ### 2.3. Flexibility

   Felines that are presented to different settings since the beginning will quite often be more versatile. This flexibility is useful in circumstances, for example, moving to another home, voyaging, or experiencing changes in their current circumstance.

   ### 2.4. Decreased Tension

   Progressive openness to various settings can diminish nervousness in felines. Acclimating them with new conditions in a positive and controlled way helps fabricate their certainty and limits pressure related with changes.

3. **Commonsense Systems for Presenting Your Feline to Various Settings**

3.1. Continuous Presentations

1. **Home Climate:**
   Begin by presenting little changes inside the home. Modify furniture, give new toys, or make raised spaces for investigation. Slow changes permit the feline to change at their own speed.
2. **Open air Investigation:**

   For indoor felines, present open air encounters in a controlled way. Utilize a solid tackle and chain, or consider making a safe open air nook. Administered outside time permits felines to encounter new sights, scents, and surfaces.

3.2. Transporter Acclimation

1. **Positive Affiliation:**
   Make the transporter a positive and agreeable space. Place treats, toys, and bedding inside, empowering your feline to connect the transporter with positive encounters. Leave the transporter open in natural spaces so your feline can investigate it at their recreation.
2. **Little excursions:**

   Go on short outings with your feline in the transporter to get them acclimated with movement. Steadily increment the length and distance of excursions, continuously guaranteeing that the experience stays positive. Reward them with treats and commendation during and after each outing.

3.3. New Individuals and Creatures

1. **Controlled Presentations:**
   Open your feline to new individuals and creatures in a controlled climate. Permit them to see from a good ways and utilize encouraging feedback, like treats and delicate recognition, to make positive affiliations. Screen their non-verbal communication for indications of solace or stress.
2. **Recognizable Aromas:**

   Prior to presenting new individuals or creatures, trade things with their aromas. This should be possible by trading covers, toys, or different things. Recognizable fragrances assist your feline with feeling more calm while experiencing new people or creatures.

3.4. Taking care of and Contact

1. **Delicate Taking care of:**
Get your feline acclimated with being taken care of tenderly. Begin with short meetings of petting, steadily expanding the length as your feline turns out to be more agreeable. Focus on their non-verbal communication and regard their limits.

2. **Paw and Nail Dealing with:**

Routinely handle your feline's paws and nails to make veterinary consideration and nail manages less upsetting. Start by tenderly contacting their paws and offering treats as a prize. Slowly progress to short meetings of nail managing.

3.5. Openness to Various Sounds

1. **Desensitization:**
Open your feline to different sounds in a controlled way. Play accounts of normal commotions like traffic, doorbells, or vacuum cleaners at a low volume at first. Steadily increment the volume as your feline becomes acclimated with the sounds.

2. **Encouraging feedback:**

Partner openness to new sounds with encouraging feedback. Offer treats and friendship when your feline resists the urge to panic during sound openness. This assists them structure positive relationship with possibly disrupting commotions.

IV. Difficulties and Arrangements

4.1. Dread and Nervousness

1. **Slow Movement:**
On the off chance that your feline gives indications of dread or uneasiness, progress all the more leisurely. Permit them additional opportunity to adjust to each new setting and improvements. Persistence is key in building their certainty.

2. **Places of refuge:**

Give assigned places of refuge where your feline can withdraw while feeling overpowered. These spaces ought to be furnished with natural things, like their bed or toys, offering a feeling of safety.

4.2. Hostility or Guarded Conduct

1. **Proficient Direction:**
On the off chance that your feline displays hostility or protective way of behaving, look for direction from an expert creature behaviorist or veterinarian. They can give customized methodologies and address any fundamental issues adding to forceful way of behaving.

2. **Encouraging feedback Preparing:**

Carry out uplifting feedback preparing to divert forceful way of behaving. Reward quiet and non-forceful way of behaving with treats and recognition, supporting positive cooperations.

4.3. Overstimulation

1. **Checking Non-verbal communication:**
Notice your feline's non-verbal communication for indications of overstimulation, like widened students, straightened ears, or tail flicking. In the event that you notice these signs, offer your feline a reprieve and permit them to withdraw to a peaceful space.

2. **Continuous Openness:**

Limit the length of openness to new settings, particularly in the event that they include an elevated degree of excitement. Steadily increment openness over the long run to assist your feline with changing without becoming overpowered.

V. Presenting Your Feline to Explicit Settings

5.1. Vet Visits

1. **Transporter Preparing:**
Train your feline to connect the transporter with positive encounters before vet visits. Keep the transporter open at home, and intermittently place treats or toys inside. This diminishes pressure related with transporter use.

2. **Natural Fragrances:**

Carry natural things to the vet, like a sweeping or play with your feline's fragrance. This gives a soothing and natural component in a generally new climate.

5.2. Voyaging

1. **Steady Presentations:**
Prior to leaving on a long excursion, open your feline to short vehicle

rides. Begin with brief excursions around the block and step by step increment the term. This assists them with adapting to the movement and hints of the vehicle.

2. **Recognizable Things:**

Bring recognizable things, for example, your feline's bed or most loved toys, while voyaging. Having natural fragrances and items in another setting gives solace and consolation.

5.3. New Homes

1. **Recognizable Things and Spaces:**
   While moving to another home, set up an assigned region with recognizable things from the past home. Permit your feline to investigate the new space steadily, beginning with a little, agreeable region.

2. **Progress Period:**

Give your feline chance to change in accordance with the new home. Bit by bit acquaint them with various rooms and regions, guaranteeing they have a good sense of safety prior to investigating the whole space.

1. **Hospitals and Nursing Homes**
   Clinics and nursing homes assume a critical part in the medical care framework, offering fundamental clinical types of assistance to people across the globe. Throughout the long term, these establishments have developed altogether, adjusting to the changing requirements of society and progressions in clinical science. This article investigates the verifiable turn of events, capabilities, challenges, and the future standpoint of clinics and nursing homes, revealing insight into their basic job in guaranteeing the prosperity of networks.

Verifiable Advancement:

The idea of clinics traces all the way back to antiquated times, with the earliest realized establishments existing in old Egypt, Greece, and Rome. In any case, these early foundations were more centered around lodging and really focusing on the debilitated as opposed to giving complex clinical medicines. The Medieval times saw the rise of strict establishments taking on medical services jobs, underscoring good cause and care for the less lucky.

The Renaissance denoted a defining moment as clinical information and logical comprehension progressed. The foundation of clinics with an essential spotlight on clinical treatment turned out to be more pervasive. The nineteenth and twentieth hundreds of years saw a fast development of emergency clinics around the world, powered by the modern upset, urbanization, and leap forwards in clinical science.

Nursing homes, then again, have a later history. The idea acquired noticeable quality in the twentieth 100 years as the maturing populace expanded, requiring particular consideration for the old. The primary nursing home in the US, the Shreveport Home, was laid out in 1901, giving consideration to older people who could presently not live freely.

Elements of Medical clinics:

Medical clinics serve a large number of capabilities, making them imperative in the medical services environment. The essential capabilities include:

Clinical Treatment:

Clinics are furnished with cutting edge clinical innovation and a talented labor force, permitting them to give a large number of clinical medicines. From crisis care to specific medical procedures, emergency clinics assume a basic part in overseeing different medical issue.

Analysis and Testing:

Emergency clinics house demonstrative offices like labs and imaging focuses, empowering the exact finding of diseases. This capacity is fundamental for planning powerful treatment plans.

Crisis Care:

Clinics capability as the essential communities for crisis clinical consideration. Injury units and trauma centers are prepared to deal with basic cases, giving ideal intercessions that can life-save.

Recovery:

Numerous clinics offer restoration administrations to assist people with recuperating from medical procedures, wounds, or sicknesses. This incorporates active recuperation, word related treatment, and other specific mediations.

Preventive Consideration:

Emergency clinics assume a significant part in preventive consideration through wellbeing screenings, immunizations, and schooling programs. These endeavors add to the general prosperity of networks by distinguishing and tending to medical problems before they heighten.

Elements of Nursing Homes:

Nursing homes, while imparting a few similitudes to medical clinics, have particular capabilities customized to the requirements of the old populace. Key elements of nursing homes include:

Long haul Care:

Nursing homes give long haul care to people who can presently not live freely because old enough related issues, persistent sicknesses, or incapacities. This incorporates help with everyday exercises like washing, dressing, and medicine the board.

Specific Consideration for the Old:

Nursing homes are intended to take care of the exceptional requirements of the old. This incorporates tending to portability challenges, mental degradation, and other age-related issues.

Private Offices:

Dissimilar to emergency clinics, nursing homes offer a private climate. Occupants live in individual rooms or shared facilities, encouraging a feeling of local area among the older.

Social and Sporting Exercises:

Nursing homes perceive the significance of social communication and sporting exercises for the psychological and profound prosperity of inhabitants. Numerous offices sort out occasions, excursions, and gathering exercises to keep occupants locked in.

End-of-Life Care:

Some nursing homes offer finish of-life or hospice care, offering sympathetic help to people in their last phases of life. This incorporates torment the board and basic encouragement for the two inhabitants and their families.

Challenges Looked by Medical clinics and Nursing Homes:

In spite of their basic jobs, clinics and nursing homes experience different difficulties that influence their viability and proficiency. A portion of the normal difficulties include:

Monetary Imperatives:

The two clinics and nursing homes frequently face monetary difficulties, with the expense of keeping up with cutting edge offices, employing gifted staff, and it being significant to procure progressed clinical hardware. This can prompt hardships in giving reasonable medical care administrations.

Shortages on help:

The medical care industry wrestles with staffing deficiencies, including a lack of qualified medical caretakers and medical services experts. This deficiency can strain the limit of emergency clinics and nursing homes, influencing the nature of care gave.

Mechanical Coordination:

While clinics have embraced progressed clinical advances, coordinating these innovations flawlessly into existing frameworks can challenge. Nursing homes, specifically, may confront hindrances in embracing and keeping up with refined medical care advances.

Administrative Consistence:

The two medical clinics and nursing homes are dependent upon severe guidelines and consistence principles. Exploring these guidelines can be perplexing, requiring critical managerial exertion and assets.

Advancing Medical care Scene:

The medical care scene is constantly developing with progressions in clinical exploration, therapy modalities, and patient assumptions. Keeping up to date with these progressions and adjusting to new medical care ideal models present difficulties for the two clinics and nursing homes.

Future Standpoint:

The fate of medical clinics and nursing homes is affected by continuous progressions in medical care, evolving socioeconomics, and cultural assumptions. A few patterns are forming the future standpoint of these foundations:

Telehealth and Remote Observing:

The mix of telehealth administrations and distant patient observing is supposed to assume a critical part from here on out. This approach permits medical care experts to offer specific types of assistance from a distance, expanding openness and diminishing the weight on actual offices.

Maturing Populace and Long haul Care:

With the worldwide populace maturing, the interest for long haul care, including administrations given by nursing homes, is supposed to rise. This pattern stresses the requirement for imaginative ways to deal with senior consideration, including innovation helped arrangements.

Patient-Focused Care:

The shift towards patient-focused care keeps on picking up speed. The two emergency clinics and nursing homes are adjusting their ways to deal with center around customized care plans, further developed correspondence with patients, and shared navigation.

Information Driven Medical care:

The utilization of information examination and man-made brainpower in medical services is on the ascent. Medical clinics and nursing homes are utilizing these advances to upgrade analytic precision, enhance therapy designs, and work on by and large functional effectiveness.

Preventive and Health Projects:

Expanding accentuation on preventive consideration and wellbeing programs is supposed to decrease the weight on medical services offices by tending to medical problems at a beginning phase. This incorporates local area based drives, wellbeing instruction, and way of life intercessions.

2. **Schools and Libraries**

Schools and libraries are mainstays of training, assuming urgent parts in encouraging scholarly development, imparting an adoration for learning, and advancing data access. This article digs into the harmonious connection among schools and libraries, investigating their singular capabilities, shared goals, challenges, and the advancing scene of instruction and data spread.

Schools: The Groundworks of Training

Essential Capabilities:

Schools act as formal foundations of training, giving organized learning conditions to understudies at different phases of their scholastic process. The essential elements of schools incorporate giving information, sustaining interactive abilities, and encouraging self-improvement.

Educational program Conveyance:

One of the center liabilities of schools is the conveyance of a balanced educational program. From rudimentary to secondary school, instructive foundations establish a climate where understudies draw in with a different scope of subjects, empowering decisive reasoning and expertise improvement.

Socialization and Character Advancement:

Schools assume a critical part in the socialization of understudies, assisting them with creating relational abilities, collaboration, and a feeling of obligation. Moreover, schools add to character advancement by imparting values and moral standards.

Extracurricular Exercises:

Past scholastics, schools offer extracurricular exercises like games, expressions, and clubs. These exercises upgrade understudies' general turn of events, cultivating imagination, initiative, and cooperation.

Libraries: Doors to Information

Data Access:

Libraries act as storehouses of information, giving admittance to a huge swath of books, diaries, and sight and sound assets. They assume a crucial part in democratizing data, guaranteeing that people, no matter what their financial foundation, can get to instructive materials.

Advancing Education:

Libraries are bosses of proficiency, supporting understanding drives and education programs. They offer a calm and helpful climate for people, everything being equal, to submerge themselves in the realm of books, subsequently cultivating an affection for perusing.

Innovation Reconciliation:

Present day libraries have developed to embrace innovation, offering advanced assets, online information bases, and PC offices. This incorporation lines up with the changing data scene, making different assets open to a more extensive crowd.

Social and Local area Centers:

Libraries frequently act as social centers inside networks, facilitating occasions, studios, and presentations. They advance local area commitment and give a space to social enhancement, making a feeling of having a place.

Shared Targets and Collaborations:

Data Proficiency:

The two schools and libraries share a typical goal in advancing data proficiency. Schools show understudies how to fundamentally survey and use data, while libraries give the assets and direction to improve these abilities all through a lifetime.

Long lasting Learning:

The idea of long lasting learning is a common ethos among schools and libraries. Schools establish the groundwork for learning, and libraries expand this by offering a continuum of instructive assets for people, everything being equal, supporting continuous scholarly development.

Exploration and Request:

Schools acquaint understudies with research philosophies, and libraries give the framework and assets to top to bottom request. The cooperation between the two works with a consistent change from scholastic exploration in schools to free academic pursuits.

Local area Effort:

The two organizations assume crucial parts in local area outreach. Schools draw in with guardians, nearby organizations, and local area associations, while libraries frequently act as public venues, offering a scope of administrations past book loaning.

Challenges Looked by Schools and Libraries:

Innovative Variations:

Abberations in admittance to innovation and the web can block the two schools and libraries in giving fair instructive open doors. Crossing over the computerized partition is a test that requires cooperative endeavors among instructive and local area organizations.

Financing Limitations:

Schools and libraries frequently face monetary difficulties, influencing the quality and scope of administrations they can offer. Satisfactory financing is essential for keeping up with framework, refreshing assets, and carrying out imaginative projects.

Changing Instructive Ideal models:

The shift towards customized and computerized learning presents difficulties for conventional instructive models. Schools should adjust to new academic methodologies, and libraries need to adjust physical and computerized assets to meet advancing instructive requirements.

Local area Commitment:

Keeping up with dynamic local area commitment is a continuous test. The two schools and libraries need to track down creative ways of associating with their networks, guaranteeing that their administrations stay applicable and open.

The Advancing Scene:

Advanced Change:

The advanced change has affected the two schools and libraries. Instructive innovation is incorporated into study halls, working with intelligent opportunities for growth. Libraries, thus, have embraced digital books, online data sets, and virtual stages to extend their range.

Adaptable Learning Conditions:

Schools are moving towards more adaptable and customized learning conditions, obliging different learning styles. Libraries add to this shift by giving spaces that help cooperative learning and free review.

Comprehensive Instruction:

There is a developing accentuation on comprehensive schooling, guaranteeing that instructive assets and offices are open to people with different requirements. Libraries assume an essential part in this by offering assets in different configurations and making comprehensive spaces.

Local area Driven Libraries:

Present day libraries are advancing into local area driven spaces. They offer producer spaces, have local area occasions, and offer types of assistance that stretch out past customary book loaning, causing them energetic centers that to take care of the assorted necessities of their networks.

B. Desensitization Techniques

Desensitization methods are remedial methodologies intended to help people survive or deal with close to home or conduct reactions to explicit improvements. These methods are many times utilized in the areas of brain science and emotional wellness to address conditions, for example, nervousness problems, fears, and post-horrible pressure issue (PTSD). The essential objective of desensitization is to slowly decrease the force of profound responses related with upsetting boosts, at last advancing a more versatile and controlled reaction.

One generally perceived desensitization procedure is Deliberate Desensitization, created by Joseph Wolpe. This approach includes presenting people to the dreaded or tension prompting upgrades in a deliberate and controlled way, permitting them to defy and bit by bit adapt to the troubling circumstances. The cycle normally includes three primary advances:

Unwinding Preparing:

People learn and rehearse unwinding strategies like profound breathing, moderate muscle unwinding, or directed symbolism. These activities assist with developing a condition of tranquility and diminish generally speaking uneasiness levels.

Order Development:

A trepidation progressive system is created as a team with the individual, posting circumstances or improvements connected with the trepidation or uneasiness in climbing request of power. For instance, on the off chance that somebody has a feeling of dread toward flying, the order could begin with taking a gander at pictures of planes, advancing to watching recordings of departures, and in the end finishing in genuine flight.

Slow Openness:

Beginning from the least nervousness inciting situation in the progressive system, people are presented to each step while keeping a casual state. As they effectively explore lower levels of the progressive system, they continue on toward additional difficult circumstances. Over the long haul, rehashed openness decreases the profound accuse related of the dreaded improvements.

Another desensitization strategy is Flooding, which includes prompt and serious openness to the dreaded improvements. Dissimilar to efficient desensitization, flooding plans to rapidly smother the trepidation reaction by overpowering the person with the nervousness inciting circumstance. While this approach can be powerful, it requires cautious thought of the singular's availability and eagerness to participate in such extraordinary openness.

Computer generated Reality Openness Treatment (VRET) is a more contemporary desensitization procedure that uses augmented reality innovation to reenact sensible conditions connected with the singular's trepidation or injury. This technique takes into consideration controlled and repeatable openness situations, giving a protected and vivid experience to address fears or PTSD.

Desensitization procedures perceive the significance of standing up to fears in a steady and controlled climate. These methodologies enable people to slowly fabricate versatility, diminish evasion ways of behaving, and recover a feeling of command over their close to home reactions. While desensitization may not take out all inconvenience, it means to make a better and more versatile relationship with the improvements that once set off trouble.

Chapter 4

Introducing Your Cat To Various People

Bringing another feline into your house is an astonishing and remunerating experience. Notwithstanding, guaranteeing that your catlike companion adjusts well to different individuals is a pivotal part of mindful pet possession. Acquainting your feline with various people requires tolerance, understanding, and an essential methodology. This guide will investigate the different advances and contemplations engaged with familiarizing your feline with a different scope of individuals, from relatives and companions to outsiders and experts.

Figuring out Cat Conduct:

Prior to digging into the complexities of acquainting your feline with various individuals, getting a handle on a few central parts of cat behavior is fundamental. Felines are known for their regional senses and can be mindful or careful about new faces. They might show protective ways of behaving like murmuring, snarling, or stowing away when stood up to with new people. Perceiving these signs is the most important phase in working with a positive presentation.

Acquainting with Relatives:

The underlying presentation ought to begin with the close relatives who share the living space with the feline. Felines frequently structure solid bonds with their human family, and building a positive relationship with them is basic. Permit the feline to investigate the home at its own speed, giving places of refuge where it can withdraw assuming inclination overpowered. Urge relatives to move toward the feline tenderly, utilizing delicate voices and sluggish developments to try not to surprise the cat.

Acquainting with Companions:

Extending your feline's group of friends to incorporate companions requires a continuous and controlled approach. Companions ought to be informed on the feline's disposition and awarenesses prior to endeavoring a presentation. At first, companions can sit unobtrusively in the feline's space, permitting the cat to move toward them at its own speed. Keep away from abrupt developments or uproarious clamors during these underlying experiences. Encouraging feedback, like treats or recess, can assist make positive relationship with new people.

Kids and Felines:

Acquainting your feline with kids requires extra thought because of the unusual idea of youths. Instruct kids on the significance of delicate and conscious collaboration with the feline. Regulate the communications intently, guaranteeing that both the feline and the kid feel great. Help youngsters to approach gradually and keep away from unexpected developments, encouraging a bond in light of trust and understanding.

Meeting Outsiders:

Felines might be more vigilant when acquainted with outsiders, particularly the individuals who visit your home. Illuminate visitors about the feline's disposition and encourage them to keep away from prompt efforts to pet or getting the feline. Give a calm space where the feline can notice newbies from a good ways. Progressive openness to new individuals and conditions will assist the feline with having a good sense of safety in friendly circumstances.

Proficient Experiences:

Felines might experience different experts, like veterinarians or custodians, all through their lives. These cooperations are fundamental for the feline's prosperity, and it is pivotal to set them up. Acquaint the feline with being taken care of and contacted delicately, mirroring the methodology it could insight during veterinary visits. Encouraging feedback and treats can make positive relationship with these fundamental however possibly distressing experiences.

Tending to Dread and Uneasiness:

Regardless of cautious presentations, a few felines might in any case display indications of dread or tension. Understanding the main driver of these feelings is fundamental for tending to them actually. Progressive desensitization, utilizing treats and encouraging feedback, can assist with building the feline's certainty. Talking with a veterinarian or an expert creature behaviorist might be fundamental for extreme instances of dread or uneasiness.

Building Positive Affiliations:

Making positive relationship with various individuals is critical to fruitful presentations. Use treats, toys, and recess to compensate the feline for quiet and tolerating conduct. Consistency is significant in building up sure affiliations, and persistence is vital. Permit the feline to direct the speed of connections, guaranteeing that it feels in charge and secure.

Progressing Socialization:

Socialization is a continuous interaction that reaches out past the underlying presentations. Consistently open your feline to different individuals and conditions to forestall the advancement of dread or uneasiness. Improve the feline's current circumstance with toys, scratching posts, and comfortable spots to make a conviction that all is good. Integrate positive encounters into your feline's daily schedule to build up the possibility that gathering new individuals is a positive and charming piece of life.

1. Socialization Skills for Therapy Cats

Treatment felines assume a crucial part in giving solace and backing to people confronting physical or personal difficulties. Dissimilar to support creatures with explicit errand situated preparing, treatment felines are esteemed for their natural capacity to interface with individuals on a profound close to home level. Creating solid socialization abilities is basic to the progress of treatment felines, empowering them to explore different conditions and cooperate emphatically with many people. In this complete aide, we will dig into the significance of socialization for treatment felines, the strategies associated with preparing, and the huge effect they have on the prosperity of those they serve.

Understanding the Job of Treatment Felines:

Treatment felines act as basic reassurance colleagues in different settings, including emergency clinics, nursing homes, schools, and restoration focuses. Their essential capability is to give a quieting and consoling presence to people confronting physical or inner troubles. Dissimilar to support creatures, treatment felines are not prepared to perform explicit assignments yet rather center around making associations through their delicate attitude and tender nature.

The Significance of Socialization:

Socialization is an essential part of a treatment feline's experience as it straightforwardly impacts their capacity to interface emphatically with different people and explore various conditions. Felines, ordinarily, may show regional way of behaving and timidity in new circumstances. Successful socialization helps treatment felines conquer these propensities, cultivating flexibility and guaranteeing they stay formed in different settings.

Early Socialization for Little cats:

The establishment for compelling socialization is laid during a treatment feline's initial formative stages. Little cats ought to be presented to various improvements, including various individuals, conditions, and articles.

This openness helps construct their certainty, flexibility, and versatility to new encounters. Uplifting feedback methods, like treats and recess, make positive affiliations, shaping the feline's social way of behaving.

Openness to Various Conditions:

To get ready treatment felines for their jobs, openness to assorted conditions is significant. This incorporates visits to medical clinics, schools, nursing homes, and different places where they will give treatment. Slow openness permits the feline to adapt to new sights, sounds, and scents, lessening the probability of stress or uneasiness during treatment visits.

Cooperation with Different Individuals:

Treatment felines should be open to interfacing with individuals of any age and foundations. Preparing ought to zero in on fostering the feline's capacity to bear delicate taking care of, clearly commotions, and startling developments. Encouraging feedback methods assist with building up the feline's certainty and confidence in different social circumstances. It's essential to open treatment felines to people with various actual capacities, close to home necessities, and correspondence styles to guarantee they are versatile and receptive to a different scope of clients.

Essential Preparation Orders:

While treatment felines are not expected to perform explicit assignments like help creatures, essential preparation orders improve their general way of behaving and responsiveness. Orders, for example, "sit," "remain," and "come" add to a treatment feline's capacity to stay cool and controlled during visits. Instructional meetings ought to be short, positive, and charming, guaranteeing that the feline partners learning with positive encounters.

Uplifting feedback Strategies:

Uplifting feedback is a foundation of treatment feline preparation. This includes compensating helpful ways of behaving with treats, commendation, or recess. Building up quiet and tender conduct assists the feline with partner positive encounters with treatment visits and communications with various people. Consistency is key in building and supporting these positive affiliations.

Perusing and Answering Non-verbal communication:

Treatment felines should be capable at perusing and answering the non-verbal communication of the people they associate with. This incorporates perceiving indications of stress, distress, or dread in individuals they are visiting.

Additionally, understanding and answering the feline's own non-verbal communication is significant in guaranteeing its prosperity and solace during treatment meetings. Controllers assume a critical part in directing the feline through these cooperations, giving consolation and backing.

Taking care of Erratic Circumstances:

Treatment felines might experience unusual circumstances during visits, like abrupt uproarious commotions or surprising developments. Preparing ought to incorporate openness to these situations to assist the feline with keeping quiet and created. Controllers assume a urgent part in directing the feline through testing circumstances, giving consolation and backing. This not just guarantees the prosperity of the feline yet additionally adds to a positive treatment experience for both the catlike and the people being visited.

Certificate and Assessment:

Certificate programs for treatment felines frequently expect assessments to guarantee they satisfy explicit guidelines of conduct and demeanor. These assessments survey the feline's reaction to taking care of, cooperations with outsiders, and capacity to resist the urge to panic in different conditions. Effective confirmation shows that the feline is appropriate for the requests of treatment work. While certificate isn't generally required, it adds validity to the treatment feline's reasonableness for their job.

Advantages of Treatment Felines:

The advantages of treatment felines reach out to both the people they cooperate with and the conditions they visit. Various examinations have shown the way that associations with treatment creatures can decidedly affect physical and psychological wellness. In medical services settings, treatment felines add to a positive and quieting climate, decreasing pressure and tension for patients and staff the same. The friendship given by treatment felines has been displayed to bring down pulse, mitigate side effects of misery, and advance in general close to home prosperity.

Building Bonds with Overseers:

The connection between a treatment feline and its overseer is a basic part of fruitful treatment visits. Overseers should figure out the feline's signs and answer suitably to guarantee the prosperity and solace of both the feline and the people being visited. Building major areas of strength for a through certain connections, reliable consideration, and clear correspondence upgrades the viability of the treatment group.

Difficulties and Arrangements in Treatment Feline Socialization:

Notwithstanding the best endeavors in socialization, difficulties might emerge in specific circumstances that require cautious thought and clever fixes. Normal difficulties remember dread or uneasiness for explicit conditions, aversion to specific upgrades, or trouble acclimating to new individuals. Fitting socialization strategies to address these difficulties guarantees that treatment felines are exceptional to deal with various circumstances.

1. **Interacting with Children**

   Communications between treatment felines and youngsters are both inspiring and helpful, offering a novel road for consistent reassurance and friendship. In this investigation of the elements engaged with these connections, we dig into the significance of treatment felines in youth advancement, the difficulties that might emerge, and systems for cultivating positive and enhancing associations between our catlike companions and the more youthful individuals from our networks.

   The Meaning of Treatment Felines in Youth Advancement:

   Kids frequently areas of strength for with structure with creatures, and treatment felines can assume a critical part in their profound and social turn of events.

Collaborating with a delicate and very much mingled feline gives kids chances to learn sympathy, obligation, and empathy. The non-critical nature of felines makes a place of refuge for youngsters to put themselves out there and foster fundamental interactive abilities.

Figuring out the One of a kind Necessities of Kids:

Communications between treatment felines and youngsters require a nuanced comprehension of the remarkable necessities and ways of behaving of the two players. Youngsters might display a scope of feelings, from fervor and energy to modesty or dread. Essentially, treatment felines might respond contrastingly to the erratic idea of youngsters. It is fundamental for approach these collaborations with tolerance, responsiveness, and a proactive mentality.

Establishing a Positive Climate:

Laying out a positive climate is critical to fruitful communications between treatment felines and kids. This incorporates picking a calm and agreeable space where both the feline and the youngster can feel quiet. Guaranteeing that the kid comprehends the significance of delicate and deferential way of behaving towards the feline makes way for an agreeable communication.

Instruction and Correspondence:

Training assumes a pivotal part in working with positive connections. The two kids and grown-ups engaged with the communication ought to be instructed about the feline's personality, non-verbal communication, and limits. Training youngsters to move toward the feline serenely, utilizing sluggish developments and delicate voices, makes a climate of trust and regard. Clear correspondence between controllers, guardians, and youngsters is fundamental to guarantee a protected and pleasant experience for all interested parties.

Management and Direction:

Close management is central during associations between treatment felines and youngsters. Overseers and dependable grown-ups ought to be available to direct and intercede if essential. This not just guarantees the wellbeing of the kid and the feline yet in addition gives an open door to important showing minutes compassion and grasping creature conduct.

Fitting Cooperations to Individual Youngsters:

Each kid is exceptional, and treatment feline connections ought to be custom fitted to oblige individual characters and needs. A few kids might be normally certain and anxious to draw in with the feline, while others might be more held or mindful. Perceiving and regarding these distinctions takes into consideration a customized and positive experience for every youngster.

Advantages of Treatment Feline Communications for Youngsters:

The advantages of treatment feline communications for youngsters are multi-layered. Past the delight and friendship that these communications bring, research has demonstrated the way that such experiences can meaningfully affect youngster improvement. Youngsters who cooperate with treatment felines might encounter decreased pressure and uneasiness, further developed mind-set, and upgraded interactive abilities. The harmless and consoling presence of a feline can make a feeling of safety, especially for youngsters confronting testing conditions.

Tending to Difficulties in Cooperations:

While the potential advantages are significant, difficulties might emerge during treatment feline cooperations with kids. Normal difficulties incorporate excessively excited conduct, the compulsion to play unpleasant, or an inadvertent negligence for the feline's limits. Overseers and grown-ups present ought to be careful in distinguishing and tending to these difficulties speedily, diverting the youngster's conduct in a positive and instructive way.

Showing Sympathy and Regard:

One of the significant illustrations that treatment feline collaborations can give to youngsters is the improvement of compassion and regard for other living creatures. Through these experiences, youngsters figure out how to perceive and answer the feline's prompts, fostering a comprehension of the significance of thinking about the sentiments and prosperity of others. These illustrations reach out past the quick communication with the treatment feline, adding to the youngster's by and large ability to understand anyone on a deeper level.

Consolidating Instructive Parts:

Treatment feline communications can be upgraded by consolidating instructive parts that line up with a youngster's formative stage. This might incorporate examining essential feline consideration, grasping cat conduct, and stressing the significance of benevolence and sympathy towards creatures. Such instructive components improve the communication as well as add to the kid's more extensive opportunities for growth.

Empowering Delicate Play:

Kids are normally perky, and treatment feline collaborations can give an open door to positive play encounters. In any case, it's pivotal to direct kids in drawing in with the feline delicately and utilizing proper toys. Showing kids the significance of regarding the feline's space and permitting it to start play cultivates a commonly charming encounter.

Treatment Felines in Instructive Settings:

Treatment felines can be important augmentations to instructive settings, including schools and libraries. These catlike colleagues can take part in understanding projects, where kids read resoundingly to the feline. This energizes proficiency as well as gives a non-critical and strong crowd for youngsters who might be reluctant or bashful about perusing out loud.

Building Enduring Associations:

The objective of treatment feline collaborations with youngsters isn't simply passing euphoria however the foundation of enduring associations. Positive connections at an early age can establish the groundwork for a deep rooted appreciation for creatures and compassion towards others. By establishing a climate that cultivates regard, understanding, and consideration, treatment felines add to the all encompassing improvement of the kids they collaborate with.

2. Comforting the Elderly

As society ages, the requirement for imaginative and humane ways to deal with eldercare turns out to be progressively obvious. One such methodology includes the incorporation of treatment felines, whose delicate presence and warm nature give solace and backing to the older. In this far reaching investigation, we dive into the extraordinary difficulties looked by the old, the helpful advantages of treatment feline associations, and systems for carrying out effective projects in care offices and home settings.

Understanding the Difficulties Looked by the Old:

The older frequently face a bunch of difficulties, including actual impediments, depression, and different medical problems. These difficulties can affect their psychological and profound prosperity, adding to sensations of seclusion and bitterness. The restorative utilization of creatures, especially treatment felines, has arisen as a promising answer for address these difficulties and upgrade the general personal satisfaction for the older.

The Restorative Advantages of Treatment Feline Associations:

Communications with treatment felines offer a scope of remedial advantages for the older. The quieting presence of a feline can diminish pressure and uneasiness, lighten side effects of discouragement, and give a feeling of friendship. Studies have demonstrated the way that pet treatment can add to worked on cardiovascular wellbeing, brought down pulse, and expanded socialization among the old. The non-requesting and tolerating nature of felines makes them ideal allies for people who might be confronting physical or mental difficulties.

Establishing a Remedial Climate:

Executing treatment feline projects requires cautious thought of the physical and profound climate. Making a helpful setting includes choosing fitting spaces inside care offices or homes, guaranteeing they are agreeable and helpful for positive collaborations. Factors, for example, lighting, commotion levels, and the game plan of furniture assume a part in upgrading the general insight for both the older occupants and the treatment felines.

Determination and Preparing of Treatment Felines:

The determination and preparing of treatment felines are basic parts of a fruitful program. Treatment felines ought to have a quiet and delicate personality, be OK with taking care of, and display a proclivity for communicating with individuals.

Preparing centers around supporting positive ways of behaving, adjusting the feline to various conditions, and setting them up for connections with people who might have changing degrees of physical or mental capacities.

Fitting Associations to Individual Requirements:

Every older individual has novel requirements and inclinations, and treatment feline cooperations ought to be custom fitted likewise. A few occupants might profit from one-on-one meetings, while others might appreciate bunch cooperations. Understanding the particular necessities of every individual guarantees that treatment feline projects are comprehensive and contribute decidedly to the general prosperity, all things considered.

Tending to Mental Weaknesses:

Older people with mental impedances, like dementia or Alzheimer's illness, may confront explicit difficulties in drawing in with treatment felines. Nonetheless, studies have demonstrated the way that collaborations with creatures can decidedly affect people with mental issues. Treatment feline projects can be adjusted to address the issues of those with mental disabilities, consolidating tactile excitement, recognizable schedules, and delicate cooperations to give solace and backing.

Advantages of Treatment Feline Associations for the Older:

The advantages of treatment feline cooperations for the older are different and expansive. These cooperations add to:

Profound Prosperity: Treatment feline communications give friendship and everyday encouragement, lessening sensations of dejection and separation.

Actual Wellbeing: Studies have demonstrated the way that collaborations with creatures can prompt superior cardiovascular wellbeing, decreased circulatory strain, and expanded actual work among the older.

Mental Feeling: For those with mental impedances, treatment feline communications offer mental excitement and tactile commitment, adding to in general mental prosperity.

Socialization: Treatment felines can act as impetuses for social communications, encouraging associations among occupants and advancing a feeling of local area.

Mind-set Upgrade: The presence of treatment felines has been connected to further developed temperament and a decrease in side effects of melancholy and nervousness.

Coordinating Treatment Felines into Care Offices:

The fruitful combination of treatment felines into care offices includes cooperation among medical services experts, office staff, and treatment feline controllers. A few key contemplations include:

Coordinated effort with Medical services Experts: Working with medical services experts guarantees that treatment feline projects line up with the particular requirements and objectives of the old inhabitants. Coordinated effort might include input from doctors, medical caretakers, and word related advisors.

Preparing Office Staff: Office staff assume an essential part in supporting treatment feline collaborations. Preparing staff individuals on the advantages of treatment feline projects, wellbeing conventions, and perceiving indications of positive or negative responses upgrades the general progress of the drive.

Making Assigned Spaces: Assigning explicit regions inside care offices for treatment feline collaborations takes into consideration a controlled and agreeable climate. These spaces ought to be effectively open to inhabitants and intended to oblige different degrees of portability.

Laying out Normal Timetables: Consistency is key in treatment feline projects. Laying out normal timetables for treatment feline visits permits inhabitants to expect and anticipate these cooperations. Routine visits add to a feeling of solidness and solace.

Carrying out Treatment Feline Projects in Home Settings:

For older people residing at home, treatment feline projects can be customized to fit individual requirements and inclinations. Key contemplations include:

Choosing the Right Feline: If bringing a treatment feline into a home setting, choosing a feline with a reasonable disposition is essential. Felines that are delicate, versatile, and alright with different conditions are ideal competitors.

Making Places of refuge: Assigning protected and agreeable spaces inside the home for treatment feline communications takes into consideration a positive encounter. Giving comfortable spots, scratching posts, and toys improves the general climate for both the feline and the old person.

Family Contribution: In home settings, relatives can assume a functioning part in supporting treatment feline communications. Teaching relatives about the advantages of these cooperations and including them in providing care undertakings guarantees an all encompassing way to deal with the prosperity of the older person.

Consolidating Schedule: Laying out an everyday practice for treatment feline collaborations at home adds to a feeling of consistency and solace. Reliable booking permits the older person to expect and partake in these positive encounters.

Conquering Difficulties in Treatment Feline Cooperations with the Old:

While treatment feline collaborations offer various advantages, difficulties might emerge that require cautious thought and transformation. Normal difficulties incorporate sensitivities, anxiety toward felines, or portability issues. Procedures for beating these difficulties include:

Sensitivities: Recognizing occupants or people with aversions to felines is fundamental. In such cases, elective collaborations, like noticing the feline from a good ways, can be set up. Also, carrying out exhaustive cleaning conventions limits allergens.

Feeling of dread toward Felines: A few people might have a feeling of dread toward felines, which can be tended to through continuous openness and uplifting feedback. Presenting treatment felines in a harmless way, for example, permitting the feline to see from a distance at first, assists work with trusting.

Portability Issues: For those with versatility challenges, changes can be made to work with treatment feline communications. This might incorporate carrying the feline to the singular's room or offering extra help, like pads or seats, to guarantee solace during cooperations.

The Job of Treatment Feline Controllers:

Treatment feline controllers assume an essential part in working with positive collaborations between treatment felines and the old. Key liabilities include:

Checking Connections: Controllers intently screen associations between treatment felines and old inhabitants, guaranteeing the prosperity of the two players. Perceiving indications of stress or uneasiness in the feline and tending to them immediately is critical.

Instructing Members: Controllers teach old members, relatives, and office staff about the advantages of treatment feline associations. Giving data on legitimate dealing with, cleanliness rehearses, and perceiving the indications of positive commitment adds to a positive encounter.

Guaranteeing Security: Wellbeing is vital during treatment feline collaborations. Overseers guarantee that connections are delicate, and the feline is alright with the climate. Clear correspondence with members and staff makes a protected and pleasant experience.

Chapter 5

Handling Unpredictable Situations

In different features of life, unusual circumstances are unavoidable. Whether in private connections, proficient settings, or everyday exercises, unforeseen occasions and difficulties can emerge, testing our capacity to adjust and answer really. This extensive aide investigates the craft of taking care of flighty circumstances, offering bits of knowledge, techniques, and functional tips to explore vulnerability with balance and readiness.

Figuring out Capriciousness

The Idea of Eccentric Circumstances

Eccentric circumstances envelop a large number of situations, from unexpected changes in plans to surprising crises. These circumstances frequently challenge our capacity to expect results, requiring fast reasoning, versatility, and flexibility. Understanding the idea of flightiness is the most vital move toward creating successful methods for dealing with stress.

Mental Reactions to Unconventionality

The human mind answers capricious circumstances with a blend of feelings, going from tension and dread to energy and interest. The manner in which people see and oversee vulnerability is affected by different variables, including character qualities, previous encounters, and ways of dealing with stress created over the long run.

Influence on Independent direction

Eccentric circumstances can fundamentally influence dynamic cycles. The strain to pursue fast decisions under questionable circumstances might prompt pressure and mental strain. Looking at how people explore dynamic in capricious situations gives significant bits of knowledge into compelling methodologies for dealing with such circumstances.

Fostering a Mentality for Eccentricism

Developing Strength

Strength is a critical quality while confronting erratic circumstances. Developing strength includes fostering the capacity to quickly return from misfortunes, adjust to change, and keep an inspirational perspective. Methodologies for building versatility incorporate encouraging a development mentality, creating solid social associations, and rehearsing taking care of oneself.

Embracing a Development Outlook

A development outlook is described by a confidence in one's capacity to learn and develop through difficulties. Embracing this attitude urges people to see capricious circumstances as any open doors for individual and expert turn of events. Systems for taking on and supporting a development mentality are investigated, stressing the job of ceaseless learning in adjusting to eccentricism.

Creating The ability to appreciate anyone on a deeper level

The capacity to understand people on a deeper level assumes a significant part in exploring unusual circumstances. Understanding and dealing with one's feelings, as well as perceiving and sympathizing with the feelings of others, add to powerful independent direction and relational connections. Methods for creating the ability to understand individuals at their core are examined, offering viable apparatuses for upgrading this fundamental expertise.

Systems for Taking care of Erratic Circumstances

Risk Evaluation and Possibility Arranging

Proactive gamble evaluation and possibility arranging are fundamental systems for taking care of unconventionality. Recognizing possible dangers, assessing their probability and effect, and creating emergency courses of action empower people and associations to answer quickly and actually when unanticipated conditions emerge.

Dynamic Under Vulnerability

Erratic circumstances frequently include dynamic under vulnerability. Different dynamic models and approaches, including the Cynefin system and situation arranging, are investigated. Understanding the elements of dynamic in unsure conditions upgrades the capacity to settle on informed decisions when confronted with eccentricism.

Successful Correspondence in Questionable Times

Correspondence is a key part in overseeing eccentric circumstances. Clear, straightforward, and convenient correspondence encourages understanding and cooperation, alleviating possible difficulties. Procedures for viable correspondence during vulnerability, including undivided attention and compassionate informing, are analyzed top to bottom.

Building Versatile Authority Abilities

Versatile initiative is a vital part of effectively exploring unusual circumstances. Versatile pioneers have the capacity to rouse and direct groups through vulnerability, cultivating development and flexibility. The standards of versatile administration, alongside functional ways to assemble these abilities, are examined.

Keeping up with Adaptability and Deftness

Adaptability and spryness are essential characteristics in dealing with erratic circumstances. Associations and people that embrace change, stay versatile, and turn when essential are better prepared to effectively explore vulnerability. Methods for developing adaptability and deftness in different settings are investigated.

Stress The executives and Taking care of oneself

Erratic circumstances can add to uplifted feelings of anxiety. Focusing on taking care of oneself and utilizing pressure the board strategies are fundamental for keeping up with mental and close to home prosperity. Systems for stress decrease, care practices, and it are examined to establish a strong climate.

Eccentricism in Various Settings

Flightiness in Private Connections

Individual connections are not invulnerable to flightiness, and successful correspondence, compassion, and compromise abilities are crucial. Procedures for exploring flighty elements in kinships, heartfelt connections, and family settings are investigated, underlining the significance of the capacity to appreciate anyone on a profound level and flexibility.

Unconventionality in the Working environment

The expert domain is overflowing with capricious circumstances, from market variances to hierarchical changes. Building a strong working environment culture, cultivating open correspondence, and carrying out spry administration rehearses add to effectively exploring capriciousness in proficient settings.

Capriciousness in Crisis Circumstances

Crisis circumstances request fast reactions and successful emergency the board. Systems for planning for and answering crises, including catastrophic events and wellbeing emergencies, are examined. The job of local area strength and the significance of facilitated endeavors in crisis reaction are featured.

Unusualness in Innovation and Advancement

The quick moving nature of the innovative scene presents a remarkable arrangement of difficulties. Adjusting to mechanical disturbances, cultivating advancement, and keeping up to date with arising patterns are fundamental for people and associations exploring unconventionality in the tech-driven world.

Contextual investigations: Gaining from Genuine Situations

Examples of overcoming adversity in Taking care of Erratic Circumstances

Inspecting genuine contextual investigations gives significant bits of knowledge into effective ways to deal with taking care of unusualness. Accounts of people, associations, and networks that have actually explored surprising difficulties offer motivation and down to earth illustrations for others confronting comparative circumstances.

Building a Tool stash for Eccentricism

Long lasting Learning and Variation

A promise to long lasting learning is a foundation of exploring flightiness. Embracing a mentality of nonstop transformation and looking for valuable open doors for individual and expert development add to building a vigorous tool stash for taking care of the unforeseen.

Looking for Help and Coordinated effort

In testing times, looking for help from others and encouraging cooperative connections are strong procedures. Building an organization of confided in consultants, tutors, and partners improves strength and gives an important asset to exploring unusual circumstances.

Utilizing Innovation and Development

Innovation can act as a significant partner in taking care of flightiness. Utilizing imaginative apparatuses, remaining informed about mechanical headways, and embracing advanced arrangements add to successful variation in different settings.

Reflecting and Gaining from Encounters

Reflection is an integral asset for learning and development. Routinely evaluating encounters, the two triumphs and difficulties, gives significant bits of knowledge. Carrying out a persistent criticism circle permits people and associations to refine methodologies and upgrade their capacity to deal with eccentricism.

Exploring the Obscure with Certainty

In the steadily changing scene of life, taking care of unusual circumstances is both a workmanship and an expertise. This extensive aide investigates the complex idea of flightiness, offering experiences into understanding, adjusting, and answering really to startling difficulties. From developing strength and embracing a development outlook to executing useful systems in various settings, the aide gives a guide to people, associations, and networks to explore the obscure with certainty and balance.

As we keep on experiencing the unforeseen, the capacity to deal with capriciousness becomes an ability to survive as well as a pathway to development, development, and enduring achievement.

1. **Dealing with Loud Noises and Distractions**

   In the high speed and frequently boisterous world we live in, managing clearly commotions and interruptions has turned into a typical test. Whether at work, in instructive settings, or during day to day exercises, the capacity to stay cool headed notwithstanding outside upgrades is essential for in general prosperity and efficiency. This extensive aide investigates the effect of clearly commotions and interruptions, digs into the brain research behind our reactions, and gives reasonable methodologies to oversee and relieve the impacts of natural disturbances really.

Figuring out the Effect of Clearly Commotions and Interruptions

The Mental Impacts of Clamor

Uproarious commotions can significantly affect mental capabilities, influencing focus, memory, and direction. Understanding how clamor upsets mental cycles gives bits of knowledge into the difficulties people face when presented to an uproarious climate.

The Mental Cost of Interruptions

Interruptions, whether visual or hear-able, can prompt expanded pressure, diminished efficiency, and uplifted disappointment. Perceiving the mental cost of interruptions assists people and associations with tending to the underlying drivers and carry out successful systems for keeping up with center.

The Job of the Survival Reaction

Uproarious commotions and interruptions trigger the body's instinctive reaction, delivering pressure chemicals and setting up the body for sure fire activity. While this reaction is fundamental for endurance, ongoing openness to commotion and interruptions can prompt negative wellbeing outcomes.

Techniques for Managing Clearly Commotions

Outside sound blocking Advances

Progressions in innovation have led to sound blocking gadgets that can really hinder or limit outer sounds. Investigating the utilization of surrounding sound blocking earphones, earplugs, and soundproofing methods makes an actual hindrance against boisterous commotions, cultivating a calmer and more engaged climate.

Making Acoustically Well disposed Spaces

Planning spaces considering acoustics can altogether decrease the effect of clearly commotions. Utilizing sound-retaining materials, key furniture position, and engineering adjustments add to establishing conditions that are helpful for fixation and efficiency.

Executing Calm Hours or Zones

In both expert and individual settings, laying out assigned calm hours or zones furnishes people with committed reality for centered work or unwinding. Conveying and regarding these limits add to a more amicable and useful climate.

Using Background noise Encompassing Sounds

In spite of troublesome commotions, background noise surrounding sounds can affect the brain. Using these foundation sounds, whether through devoted machines or applications, establishes a reliable hear-able climate that can veil irregular boisterous commotions.

Systems for Managing Interruptions

Executing the Pomodoro Procedure

The Pomodoro Procedure is a time usage technique that includes breaking work into spans, customarily 25 minutes long, isolated by brief breaks. This approach improves center and limits the effect of interruptions by making organized work periods.

Laying out Clear Work Limits

Defining clear limits for work areas and assignments limits interruptions. Conveying these limits to partners, relatives, or flat mates cultivates a steady climate where people can focus on their work without pointless interferences.

Rehearsing Care and Reflection

Care and reflection strategies are powerful devices for overseeing interruptions by advancing mindfulness and focus. Integrating care rehearses into day to day schedules improves mental lucidity and strength even with outer disturbances.

Utilizing Undertaking The executives Instruments

Advanced apparatuses and applications intended for task the executives can help people in coordinating and focusing on their work. These devices assist with making an organized way to deal with undertakings, diminishing the probability of becoming overpowered by interruptions.

Systems for Fighting Both Boisterous Commotions and Interruptions

Redoing Customized Playlists

Paying attention to music or sounds custom fitted to individual inclinations can make an engaged and quieting hear-able scenery. Organizing customized playlists that match the job needing to be done empowers people to really battle both uproarious commotions and interruptions.

Rehearsing the Specialty of Profound Work

Profound work, an idea presented by efficiency master Cal Newport, includes maintained, whole fixation on an intellectually requesting task. Embracing the standards of profound work permits people to develop extraordinary concentration and accomplish elevated degrees of efficiency in the midst of likely interruptions.

Using Breaks Actually

Vital breaks are fundamental for keeping up with center and forestalling burnout. As opposed to surrendering to interruptions during breaks, taking part in reviving exercises, for example, short strolls or care works out, adds to by and large prosperity and supported efficiency.

Consolidating Viewable Signals

Viewable signs can act as suggestions to keep on track and limit interruptions. Basic strategies, for example, utilizing a "Don't Upset" sign or showing a devoted work image, help impart to others that engaged work is underway.

The Job of Hierarchical Strategies and Culture

Adaptable Work Game plans

Associations can add to limiting the effect of clearly clamors and interruptions by executing adaptable work game plans. Permitting representatives to pick ideal work hours or giving remote work choices encourages a climate where people can make helpful work areas.

Calm Spaces and Breakout Rooms

Assigning explicit calm spaces or breakout rooms inside office conditions obliges people who require centered work time. These regions act as retreats from the rushing about, taking into consideration continuous focus.

Correspondence and Preparing

Successful correspondence and preparing drives are significant for making a culture that values concentration and efficiency. Instructing representatives about the effect of interruptions and giving assets to oversee them adds to a common obligation to keeping an interruption mindful work environment.

Beating Difficulties and Building Versatility

Creating Versatility to Commotion and Interruptions

Building strength to commotion and interruptions includes creating survival strategies and adjusting to testing conditions. Methods for building versatility, both on an individual and hierarchical level, add to long haul outcome in overseeing ecological disturbances.

Looking for Proficient Direction

People who find it trying to adapt to clearly clamors and interruptions might profit from looking for proficient direction. Word related specialists, analysts, and working environment advisors can give fitted procedures and intercessions to address explicit difficulties.

Empowering Open Correspondence

Cultivating open correspondence inside groups and networks urges people to communicate their necessities and difficulties. Making a culture where colleagues feel open to examining their inclinations for an engaged workplace adds to common comprehension and backing.

Contextual investigations: Genuine Examples of overcoming adversity

Associations that Effectively Alleviated Commotion and Interruptions Inspecting contextual investigations of associations that have effectively executed techniques to relieve clamor and interruptions gives commonsense experiences and motivation. These genuine examples of overcoming adversity grandstand the positive effect of proactive ways to deal with establishing interruption mindful conditions.

Building a Feasible, Interruption Mindful Way of life

Coordinating Techniques into Day to day existence

The way to long haul outcome in overseeing clearly commotions and interruptions lies in coordinating successful procedures into day to day existence. Developing propensities, establishing strong conditions, and ceaselessly reconsidering and changing methodologies add to a practical, interruption mindful way of life.

Laying out a Comprehensive Prosperity Approach

Overseeing ecological disturbances is essential for a more extensive prosperity approach. Integrating components like sufficient rest, ordinary actual work, and careful practices into everyday schedules upgrades by and large versatility and the capacity to explore difficulties.

Pushing for Interruption Mindful Spaces

People can assume a part in pushing for interruption mindful spaces in their working environments, instructive foundations, and networks. By bringing issues to light about the effect of clamor and interruptions and supporting steady conditions, people add to positive change on a more extensive scale.

Flourishing in a World Brimming with Interruptions

In our current reality where noisy clamors and interruptions have become universal, the capacity to explore and deal with these natural disturbances is an important expertise. This extensive aide investigates the effect of clearly clamors and interruptions, offering a scope of systems and reasonable tips for people and associations to keep a cool head. From utilizing innovation to making interruption mindful societies, the aide gives a guide to flourishing in a world loaded with interruptions. By figuring out the mental elements, executing powerful systems, and cultivating steady conditions, people can improve their capacity to focus, accomplish their objectives, and lead satisfying, useful lives.

2. **Ensuring Your Cat's Comfort and Safety**

Felines, known for their autonomous and elegant nature, flourish in conditions that focus on their solace and security. As dependable feline proprietors, making a space that meets both the physical and mental requirements of your catlike companion is fundamental for their general prosperity. In this extensive aide, we investigate different parts of guaranteeing your feline's solace and security, from establishing a feline accommodating climate to tending to wellbeing and wellbeing concerns.

Establishing a Home Climate that welcomes felines

1. **Free from even a hint of harm Spaces:**
   Felines value having secure and raised spaces where they can notice their environmental elements. Giving feline trees, racks, or window roosts permits them to fulfill their regular sense to climb and roost while having a good sense of reassurance.

2. **Open to Resting Regions:**

Felines are infamous for their adoration for resting. Guarantee your feline approaches agreeable and comfortable dozing regions. Consider giving delicate beds or covers in calm corners or regions with negligible pedestrian activity.

3. **Scratching Posts and Cushions:**

Scratching is a characteristic way of behaving for felines that assists them with keeping up with sound paws and imprint their domain. Providing scratching posts or cushions in different areas all through your home fulfills this impulse while safeguarding your furnishings.

4. **Intuitive Toys:**

Draw in your feline's perky nature with intelligent toys. Toys that copy prey, like quill wands or laser pointers, can give mental feeling and exercise. Turn toys consistently to keep their advantage aroused.

5. **Litter Box Situation:**

Legitimate situation of the litter box is essential for your feline's solace. Pick a calm and effectively open area, away from their taking care of region. Guarantee that the crate is kept clean, as felines are bound to utilize a clean litter box.

6. **Feline Well disposed Furnishings:**

While choosing furniture, think about feline well disposed plans. Feline racks, comfortable niches, and furniture with worked in scratching surfaces take special care of your feline's necessities while flawlessly mixing into your home stylistic theme.

Tending to Wellbeing and Healthful Necessities

1. **Normal Veterinary Exams:**

Routine veterinary exams are fundamental for checking your feline's wellbeing. Normal assessments, inoculations, and preventive consideration assist with distinguishing potential issues early, guaranteeing brief treatment and a more extended, better life for your catlike sidekick.

2. **Appropriate Sustenance:**

A decent and nutritious eating regimen is principal to your feline's prosperity. Talk with your veterinarian to decide the best eating routine for your feline's age, weight, and ailments. Give new water consistently to keep your feline all around hydrated.

3. **Dental Consideration:**

Dental wellbeing is frequently neglected however is vital for your feline's general prosperity. Present dental consideration schedules, like cleaning their teeth or giving dental treats, to forestall dental issues and keep up with great oral cleanliness.

4. **Parasite Anticipation:**

Shield your feline from parasites, including insects, ticks, and worms. Use veterinarian-suggested preventive medicines, and be careful for indications of pervasion. Ordinary prepping additionally supports early identification.

5. **Fixing or Fixing:**

Think about fixing or fixing your feline to forestall undesirable litters and to resolve specific social issues. This methodology additionally adds to your feline's general wellbeing and lessens the gamble of specific sicknesses.

6. **Checking Weight and Exercise:**

Keeping a solid weight is vital for your feline's wellbeing. Corpulence can prompt different medical problems. Give valuable chances to play and exercise, and screen their weight with direction from your veterinarian.

Guaranteeing a Safe Outside Encounter

1. **Regulated Outside Time:**

On the off chance that you permit your feline outside, guarantee it is in a controlled and regulated climate. A safe lawn or a very much fenced region limits the gamble of mishaps, experiences with untamed life, or openness to poisons.

2. **Recognizable proof and Microchipping:**

In the event that your feline meanders outside, appropriate ID is fundamental. A restraint with an ID tag and microchipping can build the possibilities of a protected return on the off chance that your feline gets derailed.

3. **Outside Fenced in areas:**

Think about introducing outside nooks, generally known as catios, to give a protected and encased space where your feline can partake in the outside without openness to expected risks.

4. **Keeping away from Harmful Plants and Substances:**

Be aware of the plants in your open air space, as some can be poisonous to felines. Moreover, guarantee that any synthetics, composts, or pesticides utilized in your yard are pet-accommodating and ok for your feline.

Overseeing Pressure and Nervousness

1. **Places of refuge Inside:**

Make safe retreats inside your home where your feline can escape to assuming inclination focused. These spaces ought to hush up, agreeable, and furnished with natural things like sheet material or toys.

2. **Reliable Daily practice:**

Felines flourish with schedule. Lay out and keep up with steady taking care of times, play meetings, and rest plans. Consistency adds to a conviction that all is good for your feline.

3. **Steady Presentations:**

Present new individuals, creatures, or changes to the climate steadily. Abrupt changes can cause pressure and nervousness in felines. Persistence and up-lifting feedback assist them with adjusting all the more easily.

4. **Pheromone Diffusers:**

Feliway, an engineered cat facial pheromone, is accessible in diffuser structure and can assist with lessening pressure. Setting these diffusers in regions where your feline invests the greater part of its energy can establish a quieting climate.

5. **Satisfactory Play and Advancement:**

Draw in your feline in ordinary play and mental feeling. Puzzle toys, intuitive feeders, and pivoting toys keep their brains dynamic and assist with easing fatigue, decreasing the probability of stress-related ways of behaving.

Planning for Crises

1. **First aid pack:**

Collect a first aid kit for your feline, including fundamental supplies like food, water, meds, and clinical records. Having these things promptly accessible can be urgent in case of a departure or crisis.

2. **Recognizable proof and Records:**

Keep refreshed recognizable proof on your feline, including a new photograph, CPU data, and your contact subtleties. Keep a document with your feline's clinical records, immunization history, and any important data for fast reference.

3. **Crisis Clearing Plan:**

Set up a clearing plan that incorporates your feline. Know the areas of adjacent pet-accommodating safe houses, and have transporters and transportation promptly accessible. Practice departure drills to guarantee a smooth cycle.

4. **Contact Data:**

Keep a rundown of crisis contacts, including your veterinarian's number, close by creature clinics, and contact data for companions or family who can aid instance of a crisis.

Normal Family Dangers and Wellbeing Measures

1. **Harmful Plants and Food varieties:**
   Know about plants and food varieties that are harmful to felines. Eliminate poisonous plants from your home, and guarantee that all human food varieties available to your feline are ok for cat utilization.
2. **Secure Family Things:**
   Secure family things that represent a gamble to your feline, for example, free lines, little items that can be gulped, and things that might be unsafe whenever pushed over. Establishing a feline accommodating climate limits possible risks.
3. **Safe Capacity of Cleaning Items:**
   Store cleaning items, cleansers, and synthetic compounds in secure cupboards. Pick pet-safe cleaning items, or guarantee that surfaces are completely cleaned and dried prior to permitting your feline admittance to treated regions.
4. **Electrical Line The executives:**

Felines might be enticed to bite on electrical ropes, representing a serious danger. Use line the board arrangements, like defensive covers or camouflage, to keep your feline from getting to ropes.

Building Serious areas of strength for a Through Trust and Friendship

1. **Uplifting feedback:**
   Assemble entrust with your feline through encouraging feedback. Reward appropriate conduct with treats, fondness, or play. This makes a positive relationship with your presence and fortifies your bond.
2. **Regard Your Feline's Space:**
   Regard your feline's requirement for individual space. Try not to drive co-operations, and let your feline start contact. Understanding their non-verbal communication and signs lays out an agreeable relationship.
3. **Preparing and Cleanliness:**
   Ordinary prepping adds to your feline's solace and cleanliness. Brushing their fur, managing nails, and cleaning ears are fundamental parts of feline consideration that additionally give holding valuable open doors.
4. **Veterinary Visits:**

Make veterinary visits as tranquil as could really be expected. Use transporters that your feline partners with positive encounters, and think about bringing natural things, like a sweeping or toy, to the facility. Ordinary veterinary visits support your obligation to their prosperity.

A Long period of Cat Prosperity

Guaranteeing your feline's solace and wellbeing is a continuous responsibility that improves both your feline's life and your relationship with them. By getting it and tending to their physical, mental, and natural necessities, you give an establishment to a long period of cat prosperity. Whether making a feline accommodating home, overseeing wellbeing and security concerns, or cultivating areas of strength for a through trust and warmth, your endeavors add to a cheerful, solid, and satisfied feline. As you set out on this excursion of care and friendship, the prizes of an amicable existence with your catlike companion anticipate.

Chapter 6

Therapy Cat Etiquette

In the domain of creature helped treatment, treatment felines assume a huge part in giving solace, friendship, and backing to people in different settings. As the interest for treatment feline projects keeps on developing, it becomes basic to comprehend and stick to appropriate manners while communicating with these catlike colleagues. This extensive aide investigates the subtleties of treatment feline decorum, covering perspectives like way of behaving, dealing with, preparing, and the significance of establishing a positive and deferential climate for both treatment felines and the people they serve.

Understanding the Job of Treatment Felines

1. **The Restorative Job:**

   Treatment felines are prepared to offer profound help and friendship to people in medical clinics, nursing homes, schools, and different settings. Their quieting presence can ease pressure, lessen tension, and add to a general positive environment.

2. **Separating Treatment Felines from Administration Creatures:**

   It's pivotal to perceive the differentiation between treatment felines and administration creatures. While administration creatures are prepared to perform explicit undertakings for people with handicaps, treatment felines offer everyday reassurance to a more extensive crowd. Accordingly, treatment felines might not have similar legitimate honors as administration creatures with regards to community.

3. **Determination Rules for Treatment Felines:**

Treatment felines ought to show a quiet and delicate personality. The determination cycle includes surveying a feline's solace with taking care of, flexibility to new conditions, and eagerness to cooperate with different people. Felines with an anticipated and non-forceful nature are normally picked for treatment work.

Manners for Collaborating with Treatment Felines

1. **Look for Consent Prior to Drawing nearer:**

   Continuously look for consent from the treatment feline controller prior to drawing closer or connecting with the feline. Regarding the controller's direction guarantees that the feline's prosperity and solace are focused on.

2. **Move toward Serenely and Gradually:**

   At the point when given authorization, move toward the treatment feline smoothly and gradually. Abrupt developments or uproarious commotions can frighten the feline, possibly prompting pressure or inconvenience.

3. **Permit the Feline to Start Contact:**

   Permit the treatment feline to start contact. Felines might show interest by drawing nearer or scouring against you. Abstain from constraining communications, and show restraint, allowing the feline to establish the rhythm.

4. **Be Aware of the Feline's Non-verbal communication:**

   Understanding a feline's non-verbal communication is vital. Indications of misery or inconvenience incorporate straightened ears, a jerking tail, or endeavors to withdraw. Assuming that the feline gives any of these indications, give them space and permit them to separate.

5. **Delicate Petting Procedures:**

   While petting a treatment feline, utilize delicate and slow strokes. Try not to pet delicate regions, for example, the gut except if the feline expressly shows an inclination for it. Focus on the feline's responses to guarantee they are OK with the communication.

6. **Keep away from Clearly or Unexpected Commotions:**

   Uproarious or unexpected commotions can be agitating for treatment felines. At the point when in their presence, keep a tranquil and quiet disposition. Switch off cell phones or set them to quiet mode to stay away from abrupt interruptions.

7. **Be Aware of Sensitivities:**

Prior to interfacing with a treatment feline, ask about possible sensitivities among the people present. Certain individuals might be adversely affected by felines, and avoiding potential risk, like washing hands after connections, can assist with forestalling hypersensitive responses.

Dealing with and Care of Treatment Felines

1. **Regard the Controller's Guidelines:**

   Treatment feline controllers are prepared to grasp their feline's requirements and inclinations. Continuously regard the overseer's directions in regards to how to approach, handle, and cooperate with the treatment feline.

2. **Appropriate Holding Procedures:**

   Assuming the overseer allows to hold the treatment feline, follow legitimate holding procedures. Support the feline's body safely, permitting them to have a real sense of reassurance and agreeable. Try not to limit or keeping the feline despite their desire to the contrary.

3. **Be Aware of Tangible Over-burden:**

   In specific conditions, treatment felines might encounter tangible over-burden because of clamor, lights, or different upgrades. Know about the feline's anxiety, and if essential, permit them breaks or make a calmer space for them to withdraw.

4. **Standard Wellbeing Exams:**

   Treatment felines go through standard wellbeing exams to guarantee they are truly and intellectually fit for their job. Sticking to veterinary proposals and revealing any progressions in conduct or wellbeing is fundamental for the feline's prosperity.

5. **Preparing and Cleanliness:**

   Keeping up with the cleanliness of treatment felines is vital. Normal preparing, including brushing and nail managing, guarantees the feline remaining parts open to during collaborations. Controllers might give explicit directions with respect to preparing schedules.

   Preparing and Certificate Rules

1. **Certificate Associations:**

   Treatment felines frequently go through preparing and certificate processes worked with by perceived associations. These associations set guidelines for conduct, preparing, and controller skill. Find out more about the particular necessities of the accreditation association related with the treatment feline.

2. **Progressing Preparing:**

   Treatment feline preparation is a continuous interaction. Indeed, even after accreditation, controllers keep on building up sure ways of behaving and open their felines to various conditions to keep up with their flexibility and solace during treatment visits.

3. **Controller Schooling:**

   Controllers assume a crucial part in treatment feline connections. Training on legitimate dealing with, figuring out cat conduct, and perceiving indications of stress or inconvenience enables controllers to make posi-tive and advancing encounters for both the feline and those they visit.

4. **Reestablishment and Recertification:**

Certificates normally have lapse dates, and treatment felines might have to occasionally go through recertification. Remaining informed about reestab-lishment prerequisites guarantees that treatment felines are reliably satisfying the guidelines set by confirmation associations.

Guaranteeing a Positive Climate for Treatment Feline Visits

1. **Keep a Calm Environment:**

Making a tranquil and quiet environment is fundamental for treat-ment feline visits. Limit superfluous clamor and aggravations to permit people to profit from the remedial experience completely.

2. **Give Open to Resting Regions:**

Offering open to resting regions for treatment felines during visits guarantees they have a retreat space if necessary. A tranquil corner with natural sheet material permits felines to unwind between connections.

3. **Teach People About Manners:**

Teach people in the treatment feline's current circumstance about ap-propriate manners. This incorporates making sense of the significance of looking for consent prior to communicating, keeping away from unexpected developments, and regarding the feline's limits.

4. **Address Dread or Sensitivities:**

Assuming that people express apprehension about or sensitivity to fe-lines, go to proper lengths to address their interests. This might include making separate spaces or giving data on sensitivity counteraction.

5. **Screen Cooperations:**

Overseers and people present during treatment feline visits ought to screen communications intently. Assuming that the feline gives indications of stress or uneasiness, changes can be made to the climate or cooperations to guaran-tee their prosperity.

Expected Difficulties and How to Address Them

1. **Dread or Tension in People:**

A few people might be unfortunate or restless around felines. Over-seers ought to be ready to address these worries by giving data about the feline's demeanor, permitting people to see from a good ways, or offering elective exercises.

2. **Overstimulation in Felines:**

   Treatment felines, similar to any catlike, may become overwhelmed in specific circumstances. Controllers ought to be receptive to indications of overstimulation, like expanded vocalization or fretfulness, and go to proactive lengths, for example, giving a break or a calm space.

3. **Natural Stressors:**

   Changes in climate, like new scents, sounds, or new individuals, can pressure treatment felines. Controllers ought to adapt felines to new conditions continuously and be aware of possible stressors during visits.

4. **Improper Dealing with:**

In certain examples, people might endeavor to deal with treatment felines improperly. It would be ideal for controllers to intercede strategically, instructing people about legitimate taking care of procedures and underlining the significance of the feline's solace.

Cultivating Positive Associations with Treatment Felines

In the domain of treatment feline collaborations, behavior fills in as the foundation for encouraging positive associations among people and their catlike mates. Complying with legitimate way of behaving, taking care of procedures, and preparing rules guarantees that treatment felines can satisfy their remedial jobs actually while keeping up with their prosperity. As treatment feline projects keep on having a constructive outcome in different settings, understanding and supporting treatment feline decorum becomes vital for making enhancing and conscious encounters for all interested parties. Through aggregate endeavors to maintain manners norms, treatment felines can keep on bringing solace, euphoria, and mending to people out of luck.

1. Teaching Polite Greetings

Well mannered good tidings are the foundation of positive social cooperations, establishing the vibe for significant associations and connections. Whether in proficient settings, get-togethers, or everyday experiences, the capacity to welcome others obligingly is a significant expertise that adds to a positive and amicable society. In this far reaching guide, we dig into the significance of courteous good tidings, investigate the social subtleties encompassing good tidings, and give pragmatic techniques to educating and imparting this fundamental interactive ability.

Grasping the Meaning of Affable Good tidings

1. **Social Grease:**

Pleasant good tidings act as friendly oils, facilitating the underlying snapshots of cooperation and making an inviting climate. A professional hello lays out a groundwork of regard and establishes an uplifting vibe for the discussion.

2. **Building Affinity:**

How people welcome each other straightforwardly impacts the improvement of compatibility. Well mannered good tidings convey warmth, benevolence, and a veritable interest in interfacing with others, encouraging a feeling of brotherhood.

3. **Social Significance:**

Good tidings are well established in social standards and practices. Understanding the social setting encompassing good tidings is fundamental for exploring assorted social conditions with responsiveness and regard.

4. **Proficient Ramifications:**

In proficient settings, the capacity to offer and answer considerate good tidings is a sign of impressive skill. It adds to a positive working environment culture, fortifies group elements, and has an enduring impact on partners, clients, and bosses.

Social Subtleties in Good tidings

1. **Verbal versus Non-Verbal Good tidings:**

Various societies accentuate either verbal or non-verbal good tidings. While certain societies focus on expressed words, others put significance on signals, looks, or actual contact. Perceiving these varieties is pivotal for powerful multifaceted correspondence.

2. **Custom versus Familiarity:**

Social standards additionally impact the degree of custom in good tidings. A few societies put a high worth on formal and deferential good tidings, utilizing titles and honorifics, while others embrace a more casual and easygoing methodology.

3. **Actual Contact:**

The agreeableness of actual contact, like handshakes, embraces, or cheek kisses, shifts across societies. Understanding social inclinations with respect to actual good tidings is fundamental to keep away from unexpected distress or offense.

4. **Timing and Setting:**

In specific societies, the timing and setting of good tidings are of most extreme significance. Good tidings might be normal in unambiguous circumstances, for example, after going into a room or starting a discussion. Being receptive to these social standards improves social keenness.

Showing Respectful Good tidings: Commonsense Techniques

1. **Displaying Conduct:**

   Youngsters and people gaining interactive abilities benefit incredibly from noticing displayed conduct. Educators, guardians, and tutors can exhibit considerate good tidings by reliably integrating them into their own connections, making positive models for others to imitate.

2. **Pretending Exercises:**

   Participating in pretending exercises gives a protected and organized climate for rehearsing good tidings. Members can take on various jobs, permitting them to encounter and answer different hello situations, building certainty and skill.

3. **Unequivocal Guidance:**

   Unequivocally showing the parts of respectful good tidings, for example, visually connecting, offering a veritable grin, and utilizing fitting language, assists people with understanding the particular components that add to a positive hello experience.

4. **Social Stories:**

   For people with mental imbalance or social correspondence challenges, social stories can be viable devices. These accounts give stories that unequivocally frame the means engaged with good tidings, offering direction and advancing comprehension.

5. **Visual Guides:**

   Visual guides, for example, banners or cards portraying various good tidings, can be important instructing apparatuses. Viewable prompts assist with supporting the ideas and give a reference to people learning and rehearsing courteous good tidings.

6. **Consolidating Innovation:**

   In the present computerized age, integrating innovation into showing courteous good tidings can be drawing in and powerful. Virtual situations, video shows, and intuitive applications can offer assorted and dynamic opportunities for growth.

7. **Support and Positive Input:**

   Uplifting feedback, including recognition and positive criticism, is pivotal for supporting amenable hello ways of behaving. Recognizing and praising people's endeavors in rehearsing considerate good tidings add to the improvement of this interactive ability.

8. **Continuous Openness:**

For people who might be uneasy or timid, slow openness to various hello situations can be valuable. Beginning with natural and agreeable circumstances prior to advancing to additional difficult cooperations considers a bit by bit way to deal with expertise improvement.

Fitting Good tidings to Various Settings

1. **Proficient Settings:**
   In proficient conditions, good tidings ought to line up with the hierarchical culture. Focus on working environment standards with respect to custom, favored methods of address, and the fitting degree of warmth in good tidings.

2. **Get-togethers:**
   Parties envelop a great many settings, from relaxed social gatherings to formal occasions. Adjusting good tidings in light of the idea of the get-together and the commonality of the people present is critical to making positive social encounters.

3. **Instructive Conditions:**
   In instructive settings, educating and demonstrating well mannered good tidings add to a positive and conscious learning climate. Instructors can make a culture of inclusivity and shared regard through steady support of considerate good tidings among understudies.

4. **Multifaceted Connections:**

   While exploring multifaceted connections, mindfulness and aversion to social contrasts are fundamental. Finding opportunity to find out about and comprehend the hello customs of others encourages comprehensive and conscious correspondence.

Conquering Difficulties in Educating Good tidings

1. **Tending to Social Mistaken assumptions:**
   Social mistaken assumptions might emerge when people from assorted foundations collaborate. Empowering open correspondence, giving social responsiveness preparing, and encouraging an inquisitive and conscious demeanor add to beating these difficulties.

2. **Taking care of Individual Contrasts:**
   People differ in their solace levels and inclinations with regards to good tidings. Some might be more saved, while others are active. Perceiving and regarding these distinctions forestalls unjustifiable strain and

takes into consideration customized ways to deal with instructing good tidings.

3. **Accentuating Inclusivity:**

Guaranteeing that good tidings are comprehensive and accommodating of assorted needs is urgent. People with inabilities or the individuals who might encounter social uneasiness ought to be obliged with understanding and backing.

4. **Supporting Consistency:**

Consistency is key in showing any interactive ability. Building up the significance of steady and proper good tidings in different settings assists people with assimilating the way of behaving and coordinate it into their social collection.

Genuine Application: Good tidings in real life

1. **Organizing Occasions:**

In proficient systems administration occasions, the capacity to offer a certain and considerate hello is important. This ability assists people with establishing positive first connections, start discussions, and fabricate associations that might prompt proficient open doors.

2. **Study hall Elements:**

In instructive settings, the act of respectful good tidings adds to positive study hall elements. Educators and understudies the same advantage from a conscious and inviting climate that cultivates powerful correspondence and a feeling of having a place.

3. **Global Business:**

With regards to global business, understanding and it are basic to regard social varieties in good tidings. Fruitful business connections frequently depend on the capacity to explore good tidings suitably and assemble connections in light of shared regard.

4. **Social Incorporation:**

In group environments, the act of pleasant good tidings advances social consideration. People who feel recognized and invited through smart good tidings are bound to participate in friendly communications, prompting the arrangement of significant associations.

Good tidings in the Advanced Age

1 **Email Behavior:**

In the computerized age, email correspondence is unavoidable in both expert and individual circles. Considerate good tidings in messages set an uplifting vibe for the discussion. Taking into account the beneficiary's inclinations and the convention of the setting is fundamental for successful email good tidings.

2. **Video Conferencing:**

With the ascent of remote work and virtual gatherings, video conferencing has turned into a typical method of correspondence. Courteous good tidings in virtual settings incorporate keeping in touch, offering a well disposed grin, and utilizing suitable verbal good tidings to lay out a positive web-based presence.

3. **Web-based Entertainment Associations:**

Neighborliness reaches out to virtual entertainment connections, where polite correspondence adds to a positive internet based local area. Utilizing deferential language, answering mindfully to remarks, and recognizing others' commitments upgrade advanced connections.

4. **Texting:**

In texting stages, the specialty of amiable good tidings includes thinking about the unique circumstance and the relationship with the beneficiary. Fitting good tidings to the particular stage and the idea of the discussion guarantees that advanced cooperations stay deferential and positive.

The Drawn out Effect of Showing Pleasant Good tidings

1. **Relationship Building:**

Respectful good tidings structure the establishment for positive relationship building. People who reliably practice and worth well mannered good tidings are bound to lay areas of strength for out, and enduring associations with others.

2. **Improved Relational abilities:**

The act of considerate good tidings adds to the advancement of successful relational abilities. People who are capable at good tidings are better prepared to explore different social circumstances with certainty and elegance.

3. **Positive Cultural Effect:**

On a more extensive scale, a general public that qualities and practices pleasant good tidings adds to a positive and conscious local area. Courteousness encourages a culture of thought, understanding, and sympathy, laying the preparation for agreeable connections.

4. **Proficient Headway:**

In proficient settings, people who become the best at amiable good tidings frequently experience professional success. Positive initial feelings, successful systems administration, and solid relational abilities are resources in the expert world.

B. Recognizing Signs of Stress in Your Cat

Felines, known for their free and puzzling nature, can encounter pressure because of different variables. As capable feline proprietors, it's pivotal to perceive the indications of stress in your catlike partners and go to proactive lengths to address their prosperity. In this far reaching guide, we investigate the normal marks of pressure in felines, dig into the basic causes, and give reasonable procedures to help lighten and forestall pressure in your adored pets.

Figuring out Cat Pressure

1. **The Idea of Felines:**

   Felines are regional creatures with a solid feeling of schedule. Abrupt changes, interruptions to their current circumstance, or new upgrades can set off pressure. Dissimilar to canines, felines may not necessarily unmistakably show their pressure, making it fundamental for proprietors to be mindful of unpretentious signs.

2. **Normal Stressors:**

   A few variables can add to pressure in felines, remembering changes for the home climate, new options to the family (human or creature), veterinary visits, clearly commotions, and clashes with different creatures. Recognizing and tending to these stressors is vital for advancing an agreeable and peaceful climate for your feline.

   Perceiving Indications of Stress

1. **Changes in Conduct:**

   Modified conduct is many times an early mark of pressure in felines. Watch for changes in dietary patterns, litter box use, prepping examples, or generally speaking movement levels. A focused on feline might turn out to be more removed or, on the other hand, more tenacious.

2. **Vocalization:**

   Exorbitant vocalization, like expanded whimpering, yowling, or murmuring, can be an indication of misery. Focus on the recurrence and power of your feline's vocalizations, particularly on the off chance that they appear to be more extraordinary than expected.

3. **Changes in Litter Box Conduct:**

   Stress can appear in litter box-related issues. Your feline might begin keeping away from the litter box, display indications of trouble peeing, or exhibit changes in stool consistency. These progressions might demonstrate pressure or a fundamental medical problem that requires consideration.

4. **Hostility or Withdrawal:**

Stress can impact a feline's social way of behaving. A few felines might turn out to be more forceful or peevish, while others might pull out and look for seclusion. See how your feline interfaces with relatives, different pets, or new guests.

5. **Exorbitant Prepping or Absence of Preparing:**

Changes in prepping conduct can be characteristic of stress. While certain felines may exorbitantly prep themselves as a survival technique, others might disregard prepping by and large. The two limits might flag hidden stressors.

6. **Actual Side effects:**

Stress can appear in actual side effects, like stomach related issues, changes in hunger, weight reduction or gain, enlarged students, or anxiety. Consistently screen your feline's general wellbeing and look for veterinary counsel assuming you notice any surprising actual changes.

7. **Stowing away or Looking for Isolation:**

Felines frequently look for isolation when pushed. In the event that your feline is investing more energy concealing in separated spots or keeping away from common mutual regions, it could be an indication of stress. On the other hand, a typically lone feline looking for unreasonable consideration may likewise be worried.

8. **Changes in Play Conduct:**

Play is an essential part of a feline's psychological and actual prosperity. In the event that your feline shows an unexpected lack of engagement in play or turns out to be excessively forceful during play, it could demonstrate pressure. Screen their commitment with toys and recess exercises.

Recognizing Natural Stressors

1. **Changes in the Home Climate:**

Felines are delicate to changes in their environmental factors. Moving to another home, reworking furniture, or presenting new family individuals can all be stressors. Progressive presentations and giving recognizable things can assist with facilitating the change.

2. **Clashes with Different Creatures:**

Assuming that you have numerous pets, clashes or strength issues can prompt pressure. Screen associations among creatures and address any indications of hostility or pressure. Guarantee that each pet has their own space and assets.

3. **Uproarious Clamors:**

Felines are much of the time delicate to uproarious commotions, like tempests, firecrackers, or development sounds. Giving a protected and calm space for your feline during boisterous occasions can assist with reducing pressure. Think about utilizing background noise quieting music to overwhelm problematic sounds.

4. **Veterinary Visits:**

Routine veterinary visits are fundamental for your feline's wellbeing, however the experience can be distressing. Felines might relate the transporter, vehicle rides, or the veterinary center with negative encounters. Continuous desensitization and uplifting feedback can assist with diminishing pressure during vet visits.

5. **Absence of Ecological Improvement:**

Felines blossom with mental and actual feeling. An absence of ecological improvement, for example, toys, scratching posts, or climbing structures, can prompt weariness and stress. Consistently turn and acquaint new toys with keep your feline locked in.

6. **Changes in Daily schedule:**

Felines are predictable animals, and disturbances to their routine can be unpleasant. Changes in taking care of times, play timetables, or consideration from proprietors can add to pressure. Keep a predictable daily schedule to give a feeling of safety to your feline.

Techniques to Ease and Forestall Pressure

1. **Give Places of refuge:**

Make assigned places of refuge where your feline can withdraw while feeling anxious. These spaces ought to hush up, agreeable, and outfitted with recognizable things like sheet material, toys, or scratching posts.

2. **Progressive Presentations:**

Present new individuals, creatures, or changes to the climate slowly. Abrupt presentations can be overpowering for felines. Utilize uplifting feedback, like treats or recognition, to connect new encounters with positive results.

3. **Keep up with Consistency:**

Consistency in everyday practice, taking care of timetables, and recess adds to a feeling of safety for your feline. Consistency eases pressure by giving a steady and recognizable climate.

4. **Natural Improvement:**

Improve your feline's current circumstance with toys, puzzle feeders, and intelligent play. Connecting with their regular senses and giving mental excitement forestalls fatigue and decreases pressure.

5. **Use Pheromone Items:**

Cat facial pheromones, accessible in diffusers or splashes, can establish a quieting climate for your feline. These items emulate the pheromones created by felines when they rub their face against surfaces, flagging a protected and natural space.

6. **Customary Play and Exercise:**

Empower ordinary play meetings and exercise to advance physical and mental prosperity. Intelligent toys, laser pointers, and quill wands can draw in your feline in exercises that copy hunting and investigation.

7. **Keep a Sound Eating regimen:**

A decent and nutritious eating regimen is fundamental for your feline's general wellbeing. Talk with your veterinarian to guarantee your feline's dietary necessities are met, and give new water consistently.

8. **Veterinary Tests:**

Customary veterinary tests are critical for observing your feline's wellbeing. Early discovery of medical problems and preventive consideration add to your feline's general prosperity and can forestall pressure related side effects.

9. **Quieting Medicines:**

Investigate quieting medicines, for example, home grown enhancements or physician recommended meds endorsed by your veterinarian. These medicines can be gainful in overseeing pressure, particularly in circumstances where ecological adjustments might challenge.

10. **Proficient Conduct Conference:**

In the event that your feline's pressure endures or strengthens, think about looking for the help of an expert creature behaviorist or veterinarian. They can survey what is going on and give fitted systems to address and oversee pressure.

Chapter 7

Assistance Commands for Cats

Felines, famous for their freedom and secretive disposition, are frequently not quickly connected with dutifulness preparing or learning orders. Notwithstanding, as opposed to prevalent thinking, felines are exceptionally insightful creatures that can profit from preparing, including help orders. These orders go past simple stunts; they act for the purpose of correspondence, encouraging a more profound association among felines and their human mates. In this exhaustive aide, we investigate the idea of preparing felines with help orders, the advantages it offers, commonsense parts of showing these orders, and give a broad rundown of valuable orders to upgrade the cooperation and prosperity of your catlike companion.

Understanding the Idea of Help Orders for Felines

Breaking Generalizations:

Felines have for some time been generalized as standoffish and untrainable, however late investigations and encounters of feline proprietors have shown in any case. Cats have momentous insight, and help orders give an exceptional method for taking advantage of this knowledge, testing assumptions about the teachability of felines.

Improving Correspondence:

Help orders act as a common language among felines and their proprietors. While felines impart through non-verbal communication, vocalizations, and fragrance, preparing them with explicit orders takes into consideration more exact correspondence, working with regular connections and tending to specific necessities really.

Reinforcing the Human-Cat Bond:

Instructional courses including help orders offer something beyond a method for passing on messages; they give open doors to positive cooperations and holding. Felines, similar to canines, flourish with mental excitement and responsiveness from their proprietors. Participating in instructional courses fortifies the human-cat bond, adding to a more extravagant and seriously satisfying relationship.

Tending to Explicit Necessities:

Help orders can be custom fitted to address explicit requirements or difficulties that felines might experience. From managing nervousness to exploring hindrances, these orders offer functional answers for upgrade a feline's general prosperity and versatility to different circumstances.

The Advantages of Preparing Felines with Help Orders

Mental Excitement:

Instructional meetings draw in a feline's mental capacities, offering mental feeling significant for their general prosperity. The intelligent growing experience keeps felines ready, inquisitive, and forestalls fatigue related social issues.

Changing on a surface level:

Orders can be utilized for change in behavior patterns, supporting positive activities and putting bothersome conduct down. This part of preparing is especially helpful in resolving normal cat social issues like scratching furniture or over the top yowling.

Security and Prosperity:

Orders like "remain," "come," or "leave it" add to a feline's security by keeping them from entering possibly dangerous circumstances or interfacing with destructive substances. Guaranteeing their prosperity is an essential advantage of these security situated orders.

Further developed Vet Visits:

Preparing felines to be alright with taking care of and explicit orders can make veterinary visits less distressing for both the feline and the proprietor. Felines prepared to endure dealing with are frequently more straightforward for veterinarians to look at and treat.

Expanded Autonomy:

Certain help orders can improve a feline's freedom by training them to perform explicit activities or errands. This is especially gainful for senior felines or those with versatility issues, permitting them to easily explore their current circumstance more.

Viable Parts of Showing Help Orders

Tolerance and Encouraging feedback:

Preparing felines requires tolerance and encouraging feedback. Positive encounters, like treats, recognition, or play, ought to be utilized to compensate wanted conduct. Felines answer well to positive improvements, making them bound to rehash activities that outcome in certain results.

Short and Predictable Meetings:

Felines stand out enough to be noticed ranges contrasted with canines, so instructional meetings ought to be brief and steady. Different short meetings over the course of the day are more viable than a solitary extended meeting. This approach assists with keeping the feline drew in and intrigued.

Pick the Right Rewards:

Recognizing treats or rewards that really propel your feline is critical. A few felines might favor food treats, while others might answer better to play or friendship. Understanding your feline's inclinations upgrades the adequacy of encouraging feedback during preparing.

Practice in a Recognizable Climate:

Start preparing in a recognizable and calm climate where your feline feels good. Limit interruptions to assist them with zeroing in on the orders and rewards. Beginning in a realized space helps construct certainty and decreases pressure during preparing.

Utilize a Clicker:

Clicker preparing, a strategy that coordinates a particular sound (the snap) with a prize, can be viable for felines. The clicker definitively marks the ideal way of behaving, considering quick support. This technique is particularly valuable for showing more intricate orders.

Be Clear and Steady:

Consistency is vital in preparing. Utilize clear verbal prompts and hand signals for each order, and be reliable in their application. Felines answer well to clearness and reiteration, making it more straightforward for them to comprehend and follow orders.

Regard Your Feline's Cutoff points:

Focus on your feline's solace level during preparing. In the event that your feline seems focused or uninterested, enjoy some time off and continue later. Preparing ought to be a positive encounter for both you and your feline, and it is fundamental for regard their cutoff points.

Fundamental Help Orders for Felines

Sit:

Helping a feline to sit isn't just charming yet in addition commonsense. This order can be helpful in different circumstances, including during preparing meetings, vet visits, or while hanging tight for their food bowl.

Remain:

The "remain" order is important for keeping your feline in a particular area, keeping them from entering possibly risky regions or circumstances. It improves their security and your capacity to deal with their conduct in different conditions.

Come:

"Come" is a helpful order for calling your feline to you. This can be especially significant in outside conditions or circumstances where you really want your feline to immediately return. It cultivates responsiveness and guarantees they stay inside a protected distance.

Leave It:

"Leave it" is essential for keeping your feline from interfacing with or consuming possibly hurtful substances. This order safeguards their wellbeing by dissuading them from drawing nearer or examining possibly hazardous things.

High Five/Paw:

Helping your feline to give a high five or broaden their paw isn't simply engaging yet in addition gives a pleasant method for communicating and security. It upgrades their capacity to involve their paws in a controlled way.

Down/Off:

"Down" or "off" is helpful for preparing your feline to create some distance from a specific area or surface. This can be valuable for forestalling undesirable way of behaving, like hopping on counters or furniture.

Pause:

Like "remain," the "stand by" order is helpful for having your feline delay for a brief time. It's convenient in circumstances where you believe they should stand firm on a footing momentarily, giving you more command over their developments.

Up:

Preparing your feline to bounce or hop on order, like saying "up," can be useful for empowering exercise or directing them to explicit areas. This order is especially valuable for connecting with their regular readiness and investigating vertical spaces.

No:

The "no" order is fundamental for putting bothersome conduct down. Reliably utilizing this order, alongside encouraging feedback for right way of behaving, lays out limits and imparts to the feline what is inadmissible.

Shake Hands:

Helping your feline to shake hands can be a great stunt that likewise improves their capacity to collaborate with their paws in a controlled and deliberate way. A charming and engaging order adds a hint of character to your feline's collection.

Prepping Orders:

Orders related with preparing, for example, "brush" or "paw wipe," can make prepping meetings more sensible and less upsetting for your feline. These orders make positive relationship with preparing exercises, encouraging a more helpful mentality.

Transporter Preparing:

Preparing your feline to enter their transporter on order is profoundly advantageous for calm travel or vet visits. Encouraging feedback and continuous desensitization can assist with accomplishing this, making it simpler to move your feline when vital.

Target Contact:

Helping your feline to contact an assigned objective with their nose or paw can be the reason for further developed orders. It's a flexible order with applications in different circumstances, giving mental excitement and empowering intelligent play.

Calm:

For felines inclined to unreasonable whimpering or vocalization, educating the "peaceful" order can be useful in diminishing commotion and giving a feeling of control. This order is valuable in circumstances where quiet is wanted, for example, during the evening or when visitors are available.

Track down It:

The "track down it" order connects with your feline's normal hunting senses. Utilize this order to urge them to look for buried treats or toys, giving mental excitement and actual work. A tomfoolery and remunerating order takes advantage of their intrinsic ways of behaving.

Settle:

"Settle" is a helpful order for empowering your feline to quiet down and unwind. This can be especially valuable in circumstances where your feline is excessively energized or upset, giving a way to divert their energy and advance a more peaceful climate.

Investigate:

Helping your feline to investigate on order urges them to examine their environmental factors in a controlled way. An order encourages interest and permits your feline to fulfill their regular senses while keeping up with your management.

1. **Retrieving Items**

Canines are famous for their faithfulness, insight, and adaptability as home-grown buddies. One of the significant abilities that can improve the connection among canines and their proprietors is the capacity to recover things on order. Whether it's bringing a paper, conveying shoes, or just getting a toy, helping your canine to recover things is a viable and compensating try. In this complete aide, we investigate the advantages of showing recovery abilities, the bit by bit course of preparing, investigating normal difficulties, and high level strategies to raise your canine's abilities to recover.

The Advantages of Showing Recovery Abilities

1. **Mental Feeling:**

   Recovering things connects with a canine's mental capabilities. The most common way of recognizing, getting, and conveying a thing gives mental excitement, forestalling weariness and advancing generally mental prosperity.

2. **Actual Activity:**

   Recovery exercises add to actual activity for your canine. The running, hopping, and development engaged with bringing things give an outlet to energy, supporting your canine's actual wellbeing and wellness.

3. **Bond Fortifying:**

   Showing recovery abilities cultivates a more grounded connection among you and your canine. It makes positive connections, builds up trust, and lays out a helpful powerful in light of correspondence and shared exercises.

4. **Commonsense Help:**

   Recovery abilities can be pragmatic in day to day existence. Having your canine bring explicit things, like the controller or keys, can be especially useful for people with versatility issues or the individuals who need help with recovering articles.

5. **Tomfoolery and Amusement:**

Recovery games are pleasant for the two canines and proprietors. The fervor of the pursuit, combined with the fulfillment of effectively recovering a thing, adds a component of amusing to your connections with your canine friend.

Bit by bit Preparing Cycle

1. **Fundamental Orders:**

   Prior to jumping into recovery preparing, guarantee your canine has a strong groundwork in essential orders like "sit," "remain," and "come." These orders structure the reason for a polite and responsive canine during the recovery cycle.

2. **Pick the Right Things:**

   Begin with things that are simple for your canine to get and convey. Delicate toys or things with a natural fragrance can be great decisions. Steadily progress to additional mind boggling or various things as your canine becomes capable.

3. **Present the Bring Order:**

   Start with a straightforward round of get. Throw the thing a brief distance and utilize the order "get" as your canine goes to recover it. Urge them to take it back to you by utilizing the order "come."

4. **Encouraging feedback:**

   Reward your canine with treats, commendation, or play when they effectively recover and bring back the thing. Encouraging feedback makes a positive relationship with the way of behaving, propelling your canine to rehash it.

5. **Continuous Expansion in Distance:**

   As your canine becomes OK with getting things over brief distances, slowly increment the distance. This helps construct their certainty and supports the comprehension of the "get" order.

6. **Practice Consistently:**

   Reliable practice is critical to building up the recovery expertise. Put away devoted time for recovery instructional meetings, guaranteeing that they are pleasant and not excessively difficult for your canine.

7. **Change it up:**

   Present assortment by involving various things for recovery. This can incorporate toys of differing sizes, shapes, and surfaces. The objective is to train your canine to sum up the recovery ability to various articles.

8. **Refine the "Drop It" Order:**

   Help your canine to deliver the recovered thing on order. The "drop it" or "delivery" order is urgent for wellbeing and control during recovery exercises. Reward your canine when they discharge the thing energetically.

9. **Partner Recovery with Explicit Things:**

   When your canine is capable in essential recovery, partner the expertise with explicit things you ordinarily use. For instance, you can help them to bring an assigned toy or your shoes. This adds common sense to the ability.

10. **High level Recovery Orders:**

Consider presenting progressed orders, for example, "find" to urge your canine to find explicit things. This expands on their normal aroma following capacities and extends the scope of recovery exercises.

Investigating Normal Difficulties

1. **Indifference:**

   On the off chance that your canine shows an indifference toward recovery, take a stab at utilizing a higher-esteem reward, like a most loved treat or an exceptional toy. Make the instructional courses really captivating and lively to catch their consideration.

2. **Hesitance to Delivery:**

   A few canines might be hesitant to deliver the recovered thing. In such cases, offer a similarly tempting award in return for the thing. Continuously get rid of the treat, supporting the "drop it" order.

3. **Anxiety toward Items:**

   Assuming your canine presentations dread or dithering towards specific things, present them bit by bit and utilize uplifting feedback. Partner the dreaded item with treats and acclaim to make a positive affiliation.

4. **Irregularity in Orders:**

   Consistency is critical in preparing. Guarantee that everybody in the family involves similar orders and awards to keep away from disarray for your canine. Consistency supports the learned way of behaving.

5. **Overexertion:**

   Be aware of your canine's actual constraints, particularly assuming that they are inclined to overexertion or have fundamental medical problems. Change the force and length of recovery exercises in light of your canine's age, breed, and wellbeing status.

6. **Natural Interruptions:**

   Preparing in a diverting climate can thwart progress. Start in a calm and recognizable space, continuously presenting interruptions as your canine turns out to be more gifted. This keeps up with center during preparing.

7. **Eagerness:**

The two canines and proprietors might encounter dissatisfaction or anxiety during preparing. Keep meetings short, perky, and positive.

On the off chance that disappointment emerges, have some time off and continue when both you and your canine are in a positive mentality.

High level Strategies for Hoisting Recovering Capacities

1. **Recovering Explicit Articles:**

   Train your canine to recover explicit articles in view of their names. Partner names with objects improves mental abilities and adds a customized touch to recovery exercises.

2. **Grouping Recovery:**

   Present a grouping of recovery orders, requiring your canine to get numerous things in a particular request. This exceptional procedure challenges their mental capacities and supports how they might interpret individual orders.

3. **Controller Recovery:**

   Extend the distance of recovery by integrating a controller or clicker. Utilize the remote to set off a sound or sign, showing to your canine that now is the ideal time to recover an assigned thing.

4. **Recover and Convey to Explicit Areas:**

   Show your canine to get things as well as convey them to explicit areas. This can incorporate setting things in an assigned crate or getting them to you various rooms.

5. **Fragrance Based Recovery:**

   Use your canine's sharp feeling of smell by integrating aroma based recovery exercises. This can include concealing scented things for them to find and recover. It improves their normal impulses and mental excitement.

6. **Bring in Different Conditions:**

   Sum up recovery abilities by rehearsing in various conditions. This assists your canine with adjusting to differing conditions and fortifies their capacity to recover things in new and new settings.

7. **Bunch Recovery Games:**

Draw in various canines in recovery games to energize social connection and collaboration. Bunch games can be both invigorating and engaging, cultivating positive connections among canine partners.

1. **Training with Everyday Objects**

   In the powerful scene of wellness, the combination of ordinary items into preparing schedules has arisen as a historic and open methodology. This flighty technique infuses curiosity into customary exercises as well as shows the way that one can accomplish an exhaustive wellness routine without depending on a completely prepared rec center. By utilizing normal family things, people can change their living spaces into novel exercise conditions, encouraging an all encompassing and comprehensive way to deal with wellness.

   Adaptability of Regular Items:

   Regular things have an astounding flexibility that considers a different scope of activities focusing on different muscle gatherings. Take a straightforward seat, for instance - it can act as an important instrument for lower body reinforcing activities, for example, squats, step-ups, and rushes. These developments draw in the quadriceps, hamstrings, and glutes, offering a difficult exercise without the requirement for specific hardware. This reasonable methodology advances muscle improvement as well as upgrades useful strength, working with simpler fruition of everyday errands.

   Obstruction Preparing with Family Things:

   A vital part of any thorough wellness routine is opposition preparing, which can be successfully accomplished with normal family things. Water bottles, when filled to various levels, can work as stopgap free weights, giving an adaptable way to deal with strength preparing. Bicep twists, sidelong raises, and rear arm muscle augmentations become available activities, offering a reasonable option for those looking for successful strength preparing without putting resources into costly exercise center hardware.

   Innovative Exercise routine Schedules:

   The flexibility of regular items supports imagination in exercise routine schedules. A basic towel, for example, can be used for isometric activities that target center strength. Putting the towel between the hands during boards or integrating it into curving activities adds power to the exercise, testing the muscular strength and advancing solidness. This innovative utilization of normal things not just acquaints a component of fun with the exercise yet additionally urges people to investigate different development designs, improving generally speaking actual coordination.

Mental Feeling in Wellness:

Past actual advantages, preparing with regular items gives mental feeling, a basic part of any work-out daily practice. The presentation of curiosity as normal things connects with the brain, making the exercise experience really fascinating.

This viewpoint is especially helpful for people who find customary work-out schedules dreary, as it urges them to ponder how to integrate family things into their exercises.

Openness and Inclusivity:

One of the astounding benefits of preparing with ordinary items is its advancement of inclusivity in wellness. Not every person approaches an exceptional rec center or the monetary means to put resources into particular exercise hardware. By exhibiting the viability of family things in accomplishing wellness objectives, this approach makes remaining dynamic more open to a more extensive segment. It enables people to assume responsibility for their wellbeing and prosperity without being compelled by outer variables, encouraging a feeling of freedom in one's wellness process.

2. **Recognizing and Responding to Commands**

Perceiving and answering orders is a central part of human-PC connection and computerized reasoning. In this unique circumstance, modern frameworks influence normal language handling to decipher verbal or composed directions, permitting machines to comprehend and execute client orders. As innovation propels, the capacity of artificial intelligence to perceive nuanced orders and answer keenly turns out to be progressively refined. This capacity upgrades client experience as well as assumes an essential part in applications going from remote helpers to brilliant home gadgets, making a consistent and productive extension between human aim and mechanical execution.

B. Alerting to Medical Issues

In the steadily developing scene of medical services, the combination of cutting edge innovations assumes an essential part in early recognition and opportune reaction to clinical issues. The capacity to make people and medical care experts aware of potential wellbeing concerns has been essentially expanded by imaginative innovations. From wearable gadgets to computerized reasoning (man-made intelligence) applications, these instruments are changing the manner in which we screen and deal with our wellbeing, at last prompting further developed results and a proactive way to deal with prosperity.

Wearable Innovation for Constant Observing:

Wearable gadgets have become universal in the domain of wellbeing and wellness, offering ceaseless observing of crucial signs and other wellbeing measurements.

Smartwatches, wellness trackers, and wellbeing focused wearables are furnished with sensors that can follow pulse, circulatory strain, rest examples, from there, the sky is the limit. These gadgets act as private wellbeing partners, giving ongoing information that can be pivotal in recognizing likely clinical issues.

For example, anomalies in pulse examples can be characteristic of heart arrhythmias or other cardiovascular issues. Wearable gadgets with worked in electrocardiogram (ECG) capacities can recognize such abnormalities and ready clients to speedily look for clinical consideration. This proactive checking enables people to be more participated in their wellbeing, cultivating a preventive mentality.

Far off Understanding Checking and Telehealth:

Past wearables, distant patient checking frameworks have acquired noticeable quality, particularly with regards to ongoing illness the board. Patients with conditions like diabetes, hypertension, or respiratory problems can profit from gadgets that send imperative information to medical care suppliers continuously. These gadgets empower opportune mediations, forestalling the acceleration of clinical issues and decreasing the requirement for incessant medical clinic visits.

The reconciliation of telehealth further upgrades the cautioning capacities of clinical frameworks. Patients can partake in virtual counsels, during which medical care experts can remotely evaluate their condition and change therapy designs appropriately. This guarantees brief thoughtfulness regarding arising issues as well as advances patient accommodation and openness to medical care administrations.

Computerized reasoning for Prescient Investigation:

Computerized reasoning has arisen as a useful asset for prescient examination in medical care. AI calculations can investigate tremendous datasets, recognizing examples and patterns that may not be promptly clear to human spectators. This ability is especially important for early recognition of clinical issues.

For example, simulated intelligence calculations can break down a patient's clinical history, way of life variables, and continuous wellbeing information to anticipate the probability of fostering specific circumstances. This proactive methodology permits medical care suppliers to execute preventive measures and customized intercessions, eventually decreasing the gamble of serious unexpected problems.

Crisis Reaction Frameworks:

In instances of intense health related crises, quick reaction is basic. High level cautioning frameworks coordinated with crisis reaction components can essentially further develop results. Wearables furnished with fall discovery sensors, for instance, can naturally set off cautions on the off chance that a client encounters a fall. Crisis administrations can be immediately dispatched, regardless of whether the individual can't call for help.

Also, brilliant home gadgets can be arranged to identify uncommon action examples or indications of misery, particularly in old populaces. These frameworks can then caution guardians or crisis administrations, guaranteeing convenient help with basic circumstances.

Security and Moral Contemplations:

While the joining of cautioning advancements in medical care holds huge commitment, it additionally raises significant contemplations connected with security and morals. The assortment and investigation of individual wellbeing information require vigorous safety efforts to shield delicate data. Finding some kind of harmony between utilizing innovation for clinical alarming and regarding people's security privileges is urgent for the far reaching reception of these developments.

1. **Recognizing Health-Related Cues**

   Perceiving wellbeing related prompts is an imperative part of keeping up with prosperity, and it includes an increased consciousness of unobtrusive signs that our bodies give. From actual side effects to close to home moves, the capacity to decipher these signs permits people to go to proactive lengths in tending to potential medical problems.

   Actual signs envelop a scope of pointers, for example, changes in hunger, rest examples, or energy levels. Abrupt weight variances, steady agony, or modifications in skin appearance can likewise act as significant prompts that merit consideration. Similarly essential are personal signals, as stress, tension, or emotional episodes can altogether affect in general wellbeing.

   Besides, perceiving wellbeing related signs reaches out past mindfulness; it includes developing an organization with medical care experts who can offer experiences and direction. Normal check-ups, screenings, and open correspondence with clinical experts add to a complete methodology in understanding and tending to wellbeing prompts.

   In a period where innovation assumes an essential part, wearable gadgets and wellbeing applications give extra devices to perceiving and observing wellbeing related prompts. These innovations empower people to follow different measurements, encouraging a more educated and proactive way to deal with prosperity. At last, the expertise of perceiving wellbeing related prompts engages people to settle on informed way of life decisions, look for opportune clinical mediation, and leave on an excursion of all encompassing wellbeing and health.

2. **Training for Prompt Response**

Preparing for brief reaction is a basic viewpoint across different spaces, from crisis administrations and medical care to client support and emergency the board. The capacity to respond quickly and really can have a huge effect in results, and concentrated preparing programs are intended to level up these reaction abilities.

In the domain of crisis administrations, brief reaction preparing is central. People on call, including paramedics, firemen, and policing, go through thorough preparation to deal with a wide exhibit of circumstances proficiently. Recreation works out, situation based preparing, and genuine drills furnish them with the abilities expected to survey, choose, and act quickly in high-pressure circumstances. This preparing further develops response times as well as upgrades coordination and correspondence inside reaction groups.

In medical services, brief reaction preparing is fundamental for clinical experts, particularly those functioning in basic consideration or crisis medication. Preparing modules center around speedy and precise determination, successful correspondence with patients and associates, and quick intercession techniques. For instance, medical care suppliers might take part in reproduced crisis situations to work on answering unexpected weakenings in understanding circumstances, guaranteeing a consistent and very much planned reaction when confronted with genuine circumstances.

Client assistance experts additionally benefit from preparing that underlines brief reactions. In a speedy business climate, the capacity to address client questions, concerns, and issues sooner rather than later is vital for keeping up with consumer loyalty. Preparing programs frequently incorporate reproduced situations, underscoring productive correspondence and critical thinking abilities to guarantee that client needs are met speedily.

Emergency the board preparing broadens the idea of brief reaction to authoritative settings. Business pioneers and emergency supervisory groups go through practices that reenact different emergency situations, permitting them to rehearse dynamic under tension. These reenactments assist with distinguishing expected difficulties, refine correspondence procedures, and foster alternate courses of action, eventually guaranteeing a brief and compelling reaction to unforeseen occasions.

Besides, mechanical progressions assume a critical part in preparing for brief reaction. Augmented reality (VR) reenactments, for example, give vivid and sensible preparation conditions. Crisis responders can work on taking care of emergencies, clinical experts can refine their abilities in recreated medical procedures, and client support delegates can participate in exact situations, all inside a controlled virtual space. This innovation considers rehashed work on, guaranteeing that people are good to go to answer immediately in genuine circumstances.

Chapter 8

Navigating Public Spaces

Public spaces, from clamoring city squares to quiet stops, are the backbone of metropolitan conditions, filling in as common gathering grounds and working with social collaborations. Exploring these spaces really is fundamental for encouraging a feeling of local area and guaranteeing the prosperity of different client gatherings. This paper investigates the verifiable development, plan standards, conduct elements, innovative mediations, difficulties, and future patterns related with exploring public spaces.

Authentic Viewpoint on Open Spaces:

Public spaces have a rich verifiable embroidery, developing because of cultural requirements and social movements. Old commercial centers, like the Greek public square, were not only financial centers but rather additionally puts for exchange and city commitment. Over the long run, the plan and motivation behind open spaces changed, impacted by social, political, and monetary variables. In the advanced period, city organizers and designers draw motivation from authentic points of reference while adjusting to contemporary requirements, guaranteeing public spaces stay dynamic and significant.

Plan and Engineering of Public Spaces:

The plan and engineering of public spaces assume a critical part in molding the client experience. Offsetting style with usefulness, designers and metropolitan organizers should make spaces that are outwardly engaging as well as down to earth and comprehensive. Comprehensive plan standards consider the requirements of different client gatherings, incorporating those with incapacities, guaranteeing that public spaces are open to everybody. The insightful coordination of green spaces, guest plans, and intelligent establishments adds to the general ease of use and appeal of public regions.

Social Angles In broad daylight Spaces:

Understanding the conduct elements of people inside open spaces is fundamental for powerful route. Swarm elements, social communications, and adherence to social standards impact the environment of these spaces. For example, the plan of guest plans can empower or beat social connections down. Very much positioned seats in a recreation area might work with discussions among outsiders, cultivating a feeling of local area. Taking into account these conduct perspectives permits metropolitan organizers to establish conditions that take special care of the social requirements of different networks.

Mechanical Advancements Out in the open Space Route:

In the computerized age, innovation has turned into a vital piece of exploring public spaces. Planning applications give constant data on courses, focal points, and occasions occurring inside these spaces. Savvy city drives influence innovation to improve availability and openness, making route more consistent. The Web of Things (IoT) mix takes into consideration brilliant framework, like responsive lighting and intelligent presentations, improving the general client experience. As innovation keeps on propelling, it will assume an undeniably vital part in forming how people explore and draw in with public spaces.

Challenges in Exploring Public Spaces:

Regardless of the positive viewpoints, exploring public spaces isn't without its difficulties. Packing, particularly in metropolitan regions, can prompt blockage and effect the general client experience. Security concerns, including wrongdoing and mishaps, present critical difficulties that require proactive metropolitan preparation and policing. Moreover, guaranteeing openness for individuals with inabilities stays a continuous test, requiring a promise to comprehensive plan and framework.

Comprehensive Navigational Practices:

Making comprehensive public spaces requires a conscious spotlight on all inclusive plan standards. This includes planning spaces that think about the different necessities of clients, incorporating those with actual handicaps or tangible hindrances. Slopes, lifts, material pathways, and open signage are essential components that add to a comprehensive climate. Perceiving the significance of variety in client encounters cultivates a feeling of having a place and guarantees that public spaces take care of the requirements of all individuals from the local area.

Public Transportation and Framework:

Public transportation is unpredictably connected to viable route inside open spaces. Very much planned and available transportation choices, including transports, metros, and bicycle sharing projects, add to the general network of public spaces. Supportable transportation drives, like passerby cordial pathways and eco-accommodating methods of transport, improve portability as well as advance naturally cognizant practices.

Social and Social Effects of Public Space Route:

The social and social effects of public space route stretch out past the actual climate. Public spaces frequently act as stages for social articulation, facilitating occasions, celebrations, and get-togethers that unite networks.

Partaking in shared encounters inside these spaces encourages a feeling of personality and having a place. Moreover, the inclusivity of public spaces can add to social attachment, separating obstructions and advancing comprehension among assorted gatherings.

Future Patterns Openly Space Route:

Expecting future patterns is pivotal for making feasible and versatile public spaces. Expanded reality (AR) and computer generated reality (VR) advances are probably going to assume a more critical part in upgrading route by giving vivid encounters and intuitive wayfinding. Manageable plan works on, including green framework and energy-productive advancements, will turn out to be progressively indispensable to the improvement of public spaces. Additionally, the proceeded with combination of innovation for ongoing data sharing and local area commitment will shape the eventual fate of public space route.

1. Leash Training for Therapy and Assistance

Chain preparing assumes a crucial part in the turn of events and viability of treatment and help creatures. Whether they are supporting people with actual handicaps, offering profound help, or aiding remedial mediations, a thoroughly prepared treatment or help creature can have a huge effect in the existences of those they serve. In this exhaustive aide, we will dig into the complexities of rope preparing for treatment and help creatures, investigating the advantages, techniques, and contemplations that add to their progress in their fundamental jobs.

The Job of Treatment and Help Creatures

Treatment creatures and help creatures fill unmistakable yet similarly significant needs. Treatment creatures offer everyday reassurance, friendship, and solace to people confronting different difficulties, for example, emotional well-being issues, injury, or stress. Then again, help creatures are prepared to perform explicit errands that help individuals with handicaps in their regular routines. These undertakings might incorporate directing people with visual disabilities, cautioning those with hearing impedances, or giving security and offset to those with portability challenges.

The Significance of Chain Preparing

Chain preparing is a central part of getting ready treatment and help creatures for their jobs. A thoroughly prepared creature not just guarantees the wellbeing of the overseer and the general population yet in addition improves the general viability of the helpful or help relationship. Here are a few key motivations behind why rope preparing is critical for these creatures:

Security and Control:

Rope preparing furnishes overseers with a solid method for controlling their creatures in different conditions. This is especially significant for people with handicaps who might confront difficulties in dealing with a free-wandering creature. An appropriately prepared treatment or help creature ought to be receptive to rope prompts, guaranteeing that they remain nearby their overseer and explore securely through various settings.

Community:

Numerous treatment and help creatures are expected to go with their controllers out in the open spaces. Chain preparing is fundamental for keeping up with great public way of behaving, keeping the creature from meandering, and limiting interruptions. This is particularly relevant in swarmed or new conditions where the creature's way of behaving should be unsurprising and controlled.

Task Execution:

For help creatures, rope preparing is intently attached to their capacity to successfully perform explicit undertakings. A chain fills in as a specialized device between the controller and the creature, working with the execution of errands, for example, directing, pulling a wheelchair, or giving dependability. Exact rope control is basic for the effective fruition of these undertakings.

Building Trust and Bond:

Chain preparing isn't just about control; it's likewise about building major areas of strength for an of trust between the overseer and the creature. At the point when a creature answers emphatically to chain signs, it exhibits a degree of confidence in the overseer's direction. This trust is central for the progress of treatment and help connections, where correspondence and collaboration are fundamental.

Strategies for Chain Preparing

Fruitful chain preparing includes a blend of encouraging feedback, consistency, and persistence. Here are a few successful strategies for rope preparing treatment and help creatures:

Encouraging feedback:

Uplifting feedback includes remunerating wanted ways of behaving to support their redundancy. For chain preparing, this implies compensating the creature when it strolls smoothly on a rope, answers signals, and displays proper way of behaving. Prizes can incorporate treats, verbal applause, or tender motions. This technique makes a positive relationship between the rope, wanted conduct, and the prize.

Desensitization:

Numerous treatment and help creatures need to adjust to different ecological boosts. Desensitization includes continuously presenting the creature to various circumstances and improvements while building up quiet way of behaving. This is especially significant for help creatures that might experience different conditions while playing out their undertakings. Continuous openness assists them with adjusting to new encounters without becoming restless or receptive.

Consistency in Orders:

Overseers ought to involve reliable orders for explicit activities. This guarantees that the creature connects a specific sign with a particular way of behaving. Consistency is urgent for both treatment and help creatures, as the need might arise to answer dependably to orders in various circumstances. Controllers ought to involve clear and unmistakable verbal or viewable prompts for activities like halting, strolling, or turning.

Steady Movement:

Chain preparing is a steady cycle that ought to be customized to the singular necessities and speed of the creature. Begin in a controlled climate, like a tranquil room or terrace, before slowly presenting additional difficult settings. This movement permits the creature to construct certainty and abilities at a speed that guarantees a good outcome without overpowering them.

Contemplations for Chain Preparing

While the overall standards of chain preparing apply to most treatment and help creatures, taking into account the exceptional qualities and necessities of every creature and their handler is fundamental. Here are a few explicit contemplations:

Size and Strength:

The size and strength of the creature assume a huge part in chain preparing. Bigger and more grounded creatures, for example, those utilized for portability help, may require more powerful preparation methods to guarantee protected and viable control. Controllers of more modest creatures, similar to treatment canines, ought to adjust their preparation techniques appropriately.

Task-Explicit Preparation:

Help creatures frequently have task-explicit preparation that goes past fundamental rope habits. For instance, an aide canine for the outwardly weakened necessities to explore impediments and demonstrate changes in height. Overseers ought to integrate task-explicit preparation into their rope preparing routine to guarantee the creature can play out its obligations successfully.

Overseer Versatility:

Contemplations for rope preparing reach out to the versatility of the controller. People with versatility impedances might have explicit prerequisites, for example, the requirement for a more extended rope to oblige a wheelchair or the capacity to provide orders through elective means. Preparing ought to be adjusted to meet the special requirements of every controller.

Natural Difficulties:

Treatment and help creatures frequently work in assorted conditions. Chain preparing ought to set them up for possible difficulties, like loud groups, lopsided landscape, or unforeseen interruptions. Steady openness to various conditions during preparing assists the creature with creating versatility and strength.

Wellbeing and Age:

The wellbeing and age of the creature are critical elements in chain preparing. More established creatures might require a more slow speed of preparing, and well-being contemplations might influence the force and term of instructional courses. Ordinary wellbeing check-ups guarantee that the creature is genuinely equipped for playing out its obligations while staying agreeable on a rope.

Normal Difficulties and Arrangements

Chain preparing, similar to any type of creature preparing, accompanies its difficulties. Perceiving and addressing these difficulties is vital to making progress in treatment and help work. Here are a few normal difficulties and powerful arrangements:

Pulling on the Chain:

Pulling is a typical issue during chain preparing, especially for more grounded or more fiery creatures. To address pulling, controllers can utilize procedures, for example, halting and trusting that the creature will deliver pressure on the rope prior to proceeding. Predictable support of free chain strolling with remunerations assists the creature with figuring out the ideal way of behaving.

Interruptions and Reactivity:

Creatures, particularly those in treatment jobs, may experience different interruptions that can prompt reactivity. Desensitization and counterconditioning can be utilized to continuously adapt the creature to interruptions while building up quiet way of behaving. Presenting controlled interruptions during instructional meetings helps fabricate the creature's concentration and restraint.

Tension and Dread:

A few creatures might encounter uneasiness or dread, particularly in new conditions. Overseers ought to make a positive relationship with the rope by utilizing treats, recognition, and prizes. Steady openness to new settings and encounters, matched with uplifting feedback, helps assemble the creature's certainty and decreases tension.

Overstimulation:

Treatment creatures, specifically, may confront overstimulation in swarmed or loud conditions. Instructional meetings ought to step by step increment in intricacy, permitting the creature to adjust to various degrees of excitement. Controllers can utilize quieting procedures, for example, giving a peaceful space or diverting the creature's concentration, to oversee overstimulation.

1. **Getting Comfortable with a Harness**

    Acquainting an outfit with your pet is a vital stage in guaranteeing their security, solace, and prosperity. Whether you have a canine, feline, or other little creature, adjusting them to a tackle is a slow cycle that requires persistence and uplifting feedback. In this extensive aide, we will investigate the explanations behind utilizing an outfit, the advantages it offers, and the bit by bit course of getting your pet familiar with wearing one.

Why Utilize a Saddle?

Prior to digging into the preparation cycle, understanding the explanations for involving a bridle for your pet is fundamental. Not at all like conventional collars, bridles convey pressure all the more equally across the body, diminishing the gamble of injury or stress on the neck. Here are a few vital motivations to think about utilizing an outfit:

Wellbeing and Control:

A tackle gives better command over your pet, particularly in the event that they will quite often pull on the rope during strolls. This is especially significant for canines that might have respiratory issues or neck responsive qualities.

Anticipation of Getaways:

A few pets, particularly felines, can be proficient at getting out of restraints. A tackle offers a safer fit, limiting the possibilities of your pet evading during open air exercises.

Solace and Backing:

Tackles are intended to be agreeable for pets, circulating strain across the chest and shoulders as opposed to the neck. This is particularly valuable for more modest varieties or those with respiratory worries.

Preparing Help:

Outfits can act as significant apparatuses in preparing your pet. They give a place of control and can be utilized for redirection, showing chain habits, and putting bothersome ways of behaving down.

Picking the Right Outfit

Prior to starting the preparation interaction, guarantee that you have the right tackle for your pet. Think about the size, type, and materials of the bridle to guarantee a legitimate fit and greatest solace. There are different kinds of bridles, remembering step-for, above, and vest-style outfits, each fit to various necessities and inclinations.

Measure Your Pet:

Precise estimations are significant for choosing the right size. Measure your pet's chest bigness and neck periphery to decide the proper bridle size. Most outfits accompany size outlines given by the maker to direct you in choosing the right size.

Pick the Right Sort:

Different tackle styles suit various pets and exercises. For instance, step-in outfits are not difficult to put on and ideal for pets that might be delicate to having something set over their heads. Above saddles give more control and are appropriate for dynamic pets.

Think about Materials:

Bridles come in different materials, including nylon, cross section, and calfskin. Consider your pet's solace and any potential skin responsive qualities while picking a bridle material. A few pets might favor the lightweight feel of a lattice bridle, while others might be more agreeable in a cushioned nylon plan.

Flexibility:

Guarantee that the saddle is customizable to oblige your pet's development or changes in weight. An appropriately changed bridle ought to be cozy however not excessively close, taking into consideration agreeable development without the gamble of sneaking off.

Bit by bit Preparing Cycle

Since you have the right outfit for your pet, now is the ideal time to begin the preparation interaction. Recollect that persistence and encouraging feedback are critical to making this experience charming for your pet.

Presentation and Acclimation:

Start by permitting your pet to get comfortable with the outfit in a harmless climate. Place the tackle close to your pet's dozing region or leave it out where they can examine it at their own speed. This makes positive relationship with the outfit.

Positive Affiliations:

Partner the presence of the outfit with positive encounters. Offer treats, recognition, or recess at whatever point your pet shows interest in or communicates with the outfit. This helps construct a positive affiliation and lessens any nervousness or wavering.

Contact Refinement:

Bit by bit acquaint your pet with the vibe of having the tackle contacted and set close to their body. Utilize delicate strokes and acclaim to console them. In the event that your pet appears to be agreeable, you can advance to hanging the tackle freely over their back for brief lengths.

Reward-Based Preparing:

Use treats or most loved toys to remunerate your pet for permitting you to contact them with the tackle. Reward-based preparing builds up certain way of behaving and makes an association between the saddle and positive encounters.

Step At work Practice:

On the off chance that you're involving a stage at work, practice the means of venturing into the outfit without securing it. Permit your pet to become familiar with the vibe of having their legs put through the openings. Once more, reward positive way of behaving with treats and commendation.

Steady Affixing:

When your pet is OK with the bridle around their body, bit by bit present the most common way of attaching it. Begin by getting each lock in turn, permitting your pet to change in accordance with the sensation. Keep offering prizes and uplifting feedback in the meantime.

Short Strolls Inside:

Prior to wandering outside, practice short strolls inside to permit your pet to adapt to the vibe of strolling with the tackle. Use treats and support to propel them during these underlying indoor strolls.

Progress to Outside Conditions:

When your pet is OK with the tackle inside, step by step change to open air conditions. Begin with natural environmental factors and calm regions to limit expected stressors. Increment the span and intricacy of strolls as your pet increases certainty.

Steady Uplifting feedback:

All through the preparation interaction and progressing utilization of the outfit, keep up with predictable encouraging feedback. Reward your pet for good way of behaving, whether it's strolling smoothly on the rope or permitting the saddle to be placed on. This support fabricates a positive relationship with wearing the outfit.

Investigating and Normal Difficulties

While most pets adjust well to saddle preparing, there might be difficulties en route. Here are a few normal issues and how to address them:

Obstruction or Dread:

On the off chance that your pet shows opposition or dread during the preparation interaction, make a stride back and continue all the more leisurely. Offer treats and consolation to make positive affiliations, and try not to drive the bridle on your pet.

Getting away or Slipping:

Guarantee that the saddle is appropriately acclimated to forestall slipping or getting away. Check the fit consistently, particularly assuming that your pet is as yet developing. On the off chance that your pet reliably attempts to escape, think about attempting an alternate style of tackle or talking with an expert coach.

Scraping or Uneasiness:

Screen your pet for any indications of scraping or uneasiness, particularly in regions where the bridle rubs against the skin. Change the fit depending on the situation, and think about utilizing a bridle with cushioning to decrease grating.

Overexcitement:

A few pets might turn out to be excessively invigorated when the saddle is presented, making it trying to put on. Practice quiet conduct by compensating your pet for tolerance and bit by bit broadening the time between putting on the tackle and beginning the walk.

2. Walking Confidently in Public

Strolling your canine openly is something other than a daily practice; it's a chance to reinforce the connection among you and your fuzzy friend while likewise exploring the common spaces of your local area. Accomplishing trust out in the open strolling upgrades your canine's interactive abilities as well as adds to a positive encounter for both you and people around you. In this exhaustive aide, we will investigate the critical components of strolling certainly openly, including rope manners, social way of behaving, and viable preparation methods to guarantee an agreeable and pleasant experience.

Significance of Strolling Without hesitation In broad daylight

Strolling without hesitation in broad daylight is fundamental in light of multiple factors, helping both your canine and the local area at large:

Wellbeing:

A certain and polite canine is less inclined to present dangers to themselves, their overseer, or others out in the open spaces. This incorporates keeping away from ways of behaving like over the top pulling, rushing, or responding adversely to different canines or individuals.

Positive Socialization:

Customary openness to different conditions, individuals, and creatures is critical for a canine's socialization. Sure strolling permits your canine to experience new boosts, cultivating positive affiliations and diminishing the probability of dread or uneasiness in various circumstances.

Local area Agreement:

Thought for others out in the open spaces adds to a positive local area experience. Canines that walk unhesitatingly and considerately on a chain are less inclined to upset neighbors, people on foot, or different pets, advancing a feeling of local area concordance.

Improved Bond:

The common experience of strolling unhesitatingly out in the open reinforces the connection among you and your canine. Collectively, you explore different conditions, and your canine figures out how to trust and seek you for direction.

Rope Decorum: The Groundwork of Certain Strolling

Rope decorum is the foundation of strolling with certainty openly. It includes both the overseer's capacity to deal with the chain really and the canine's responsiveness to rope signals. Here are fundamental components of rope decorum:

Legitimate Fit and Length:

Guarantee that your canine's choker or outfit fits cozily however easily, and pick a proper rope length. A standard rope length of 4 to 6 feet takes into consideration an equilibrium between control and opportunity. Retractable chains, while famous, may think twice about and are not generally appropriate for certain open strolling.

Free Chain Strolling:

Help your canine to stroll on a free rope, significance there is no strain in the chain while strolling close to you. Support this way of behaving with treats and recognition. On the off chance that your canine pulls, quit strolling and hang tight for them to get back to your side prior to proceeding.

Situating:

Train your canine to reliably stroll on one side. This makes it simpler for you to explore through swarms and keep up with control. Pick the side that feels generally great for you, and be reliable in supporting this situation during strolls.

Rope Taking care of:

Hold the rope in a manner that gives control without making uneasiness your canine. Try not to fold the chain over your hand or fingers, as this can prompt injury in the event of unexpected developments. An agreeable grasp takes into consideration fast and exact reactions to your canine's way of behaving.

Know about Your Environmental elements:

Remain caution to your current circumstance, expecting possible interruptions or difficulties. This incorporates monitoring different canines, walkers, and expected perils. By proactively dealing with your canine's responses, you can keep a quiet and sure disposition.

Social Way of behaving and Cooperation

Sure strolling in broad daylight stretches out past rope decorum; it likewise includes positive social way of behaving and associations. Think about the accompanying parts of encouraging positive socialization:

Canine to-Canine Cooperations:

Not all canines are outgoing people, and some might like to stay away. Focus on your canine's non-verbal communication and regard their solace level. Permit positive cooperations with different canines when the two players are willing, and be ready to divert your canine if necessary.

Individuals Connection:

Energize positive associations between your canine and individuals. This incorporates training your canine to approach smoothly, without hopping or over the top fervor. Give treats to acceptable conduct and utilize uplifting feedback to construct positive relationship with meeting new individuals.

Youngsters and Different Creatures:

Practice alert while acquainting your canine with kids or different creatures. Youngsters ought to be instructed to move toward canines consciously, and your canine ought to be alright with these associations. Assuming your canine gives indications of distress, give distance or divert their consideration.

Preparing for Interruptions:

Train your canine to stay engaged and responsive despite interruptions. This can incorporate openness to different improvements like bikes, skateboards, clearly clamors, and different creatures. Slowly increment the trouble level of interruptions during instructional meetings to assemble your canine's certainty.

Encouraging feedback:

Reliably utilize encouraging feedback to remunerate wanted conduct during strolls. Treats, commendation, and love act as strong inspirations for your canine to rehash ways of behaving that add to a positive strolling experience.

Preparing Procedures for Sure Strolling

Accomplishing sure strolling in broad daylight includes devoted preparing endeavors. Here are a few powerful procedures to integrate into your preparation routine:

Fundamental Dutifulness Orders:

Guarantee your canine answers dependably to fundamental orders, for example, "sit," "remain," "heel," and "come." These orders act as the establishment for compelling correspondence during strolls. Standard support of fundamental submission fabricates a responsive and certain canine.

Desensitization and Counterconditioning:

Continuously open your canine to different improvements, conditions, and circumstances. Use desensitization and counterconditioning methods to diminish tension or dread related with explicit triggers. This might include presenting your canine to bit by bit expanding levels of improvements while compensating quiet way of behaving.

Center Activities:

Train your canine to keep up with center around you during strolls. Use treats, toys, or verbal signals to divert their consideration back to you when confronted with interruptions. This helps construct major areas of strength for an and urges your canine to seek you for direction.

Organized Strolls:

Integrate organized strolls into your everyday practice, where your canine strolls serenely next to you. Utilize a steady speed, and build up free chain strolling. Organized strolls give an open door to your canine to take part in certain way of behaving while at the same time keeping a controlled climate.

Positive Openness to Public Spaces:

Step by step acquaint your canine with different public spaces. Begin with calmer regions and logically increment the degree of excitement. Positive openness to various conditions assists your canine with turning out to be more versatile and certain about different settings.

Proficient Instructional courses:

Consider signing up for proficient instructional courses, particularly assuming you experience explicit difficulties or ways of behaving that require master direction. Proficient mentors can give customized guidance and organized preparing plans custom-made to your canine's necessities.

Normal Difficulties and Arrangements

Indeed, even with cautious preparation, difficulties might emerge during public strolls. Here are a few normal difficulties and compelling arrangements:

Chain Reactivity:

On the off chance that your canine displays responsive conduct on the rope, for example, yapping or rushing at different canines, practice distance the board. Steadily increment the separation from the trigger while remunerating quiet way of behaving. Look for proficient direction assuming that reactivity perseveres.

Dread or Uneasiness:

Canines might display dread or uneasiness in specific circumstances. Distinguish triggers and use desensitization and counterconditioning methods to assemble positive affiliations. Make a place of refuge for your canine and try not to compel them into awkward circumstances.

Exorbitant Energy:

On the off chance that your canine ends up being excessively invigorated during strolls, practice drive control works out. Use orders like "sit" or "remain" prior to going across roads or moving toward different canines. Build up quiet way of behaving with treats and acclaim.

Pulling on the Rope:

In the event that your canine reliably pulls on the rope, quit strolling and sit tight for them to get back to your side. Build up free rope strolling with treats and acclaim. Consider utilizing a front-cut bridle to beat pulling down.

Interruptions:

Canines might be quickly drawn offtrack during strolls. Utilize high-esteem treats to recover your canine's consideration, and practice center activities. Steadily increment the degree of interruptions during instructional courses to construct your canine's flexibility.

Chapter 9

Connecting with Organizations

In the unique scene of our interconnected world, manufacturing significant associations with associations is fundamental for self-awareness, proficient turn of events, and local area influence. Whether you are a singular looking for help, a business person going for the gold, a local area pioneer taking a stab at positive change, interfacing with associations can be an extraordinary excursion. This complete aide investigates the complexities of building organizations, encouraging connections, and utilizing aggregate endeavors for a common perspective.

Grasping the Significance of Association

1.1 The Force of Coordinated effort

In the present mind boggling and quick moving world, joint effort has turned into a foundation for development and progress. Associations, whether non-benefit, for-benefit, or legislative, frequently have exceptional assets, mastery, and organizations that, when joined, can address difficulties all the more actually. By interfacing with associations, people and substances can pool their assets, share information, and intensify their effect.

1.2 Individual and Expert Development

For people, associating with associations goes past systems administration; it presents open doors for individual and expert development. Drawing in with similar associations permits people to get to mentorship, instructive assets, and professional success open doors. The trading of thoughts and abilities among people and associations encourages a powerful environment of learning and improvement.

1.3 Social Effect and Local area Improvement

Associations assume a significant part in driving social change and local area improvement. By lining up with associations that share normal qualities and objectives, people and networks can all in all address social, natural, and monetary difficulties. Building associations with associations empowers the formation of manageable drives that decidedly affect society.

Recognizing Your Goals and Values

2.1 Characterizing Your Motivation

Prior to setting out on the excursion of interfacing with associations, characterizing your targets and purpose is pivotal. Whether you are a singular looking for self-improvement, a business person investigating coordinated effort, or a local area pioneer pushing for change, explaining your objectives gives a guide to viable commitment.

2.2 Adjusting Values

Fruitful associations with associations frequently rely on shared values. At the point when your qualities line up with those of an association, the potential for a significant and enduring organization increments. Consider what values make the biggest difference to you, and look for associations that show a pledge to comparative standards.

2.3 Distinguishing Objective Associations

The tremendous scene of associations requires an insightful way to deal with distinguish those that line up with your targets. Research expected accomplices, survey their statements of purpose, past tasks, and hierarchical culture. Comprehend the effect they have had and the qualities they maintain. This tirelessness will assist you with distinguishing associations that reverberate with your motivation.

Methodologies for Associating with Associations

3.1 Systems administration and Relationship Building

Organizing is the foundation of associating with associations. Go to industry occasions, gatherings, and systems administration meetings to meet agents from different associations. Laying out certified associations with people inside associations can open ways to significant joint efforts. Routinely go to occasions or join proficient gatherings applicable to your field of interest.

3.2 Web-based Stages and Virtual Entertainment

In the computerized age, online stages and web-based entertainment assume a pivotal part in associating people with associations. Use stages like LinkedIn, Twitter, and expert gatherings to follow and draw in with associations of interest. Partake in web-based conversations, share bits of knowledge, and express certified interest in crafted by associations you appreciate.

3.3 Using Special interactions

Special interactions can be strong impetuses for associating with associations. Influence your current organization to look for presentations or proposals.

Individual references frequently convey huge weight and can give a significant passage highlight starting discussions with associations.

3.4 Going to Occasions and Gatherings

Partaking in occasions and meetings pertinent to your field of interest sets out open doors to associate with associations firsthand. Go to board conversations, studios, and systems administration meetings to draw in with agents from different associations. Get ready smart inquiries and effectively partake in conversations to have an enduring effect.

Starting and Sustaining Associations

4.1 Making a Convincing Presentation

The initial feeling is pivotal while contacting associations. Make a compact and convincing presentation that imparts what your identity is, your inclinations, and the reason behind interfacing. Obviously expressive how your objectives line up with the association's main goal and values. Tailor first experience with feature shared goals.

4.2 Utilizing Instructive Meetings

Mentioning educational meetings can be a viable methodology for acquiring further experiences into an association. Look for valuable chances to associate with agents for casual conversations about their work, difficulties, and future drives. This exhibits your certified interest as well as gives a stage to building compatibility.

4.3 Exhibiting Incentive

Obviously impart the incentive you offer that would be useful. Whether it's your abilities, skill, or one of a kind viewpoint, associations are bound to draw in when they see unmistakable advantages in the association. Exhibit explicit instances of how your coordinated effort can add to their objectives.

4.4 Structure and Keeping up with Connections

Building associations is definitely not a one-time exertion; it requires progressing relationship building. Remain drew in with associations by going to their occasions, taking part in conversations, and remaining informed about their exercises. Routinely express your help for their drives and search for potential chances to contribute.

Cooperative Drives and Undertakings

5.1 Investigating Cooperation Open doors

When an association is laid out, investigate potential cooperation open doors. This could include joint undertakings, associations, or shared drives.

Survey regions where your abilities or assets supplement those of the association, making a commonly helpful joint effort.

5.2 Making Recommendations and Arrangements

While proposing cooperative drives, guarantee lucidity in your recommendations. Obviously frame the targets, scope, and anticipated results of the cooperation. Draft formal arrangements that detail the jobs, obligations, and commitments of each party. A clear cut understanding sets the establishment for a fruitful organization.

5.3 Laying out Clear Correspondence Channels

Powerful correspondence is basic for the progress of cooperative tasks. Lay out clear correspondence channels and conventions, it are educated and adjusted to guarantee that all partners. Normal registrations, progress reports, and input meetings add to a straightforward and productive cooperation.

5.4 Overseeing Assumptions

Straightforward correspondence reaches out to overseeing assumptions. Obviously convey the assumptions for the two players in regards to courses of events, expectations, and any possible difficulties. This proactive methodology forestalls errors and encourages a cooperative climate in view of trust and common comprehension.

Supporting and Scaling Associations

6.1 Assessing Effect and Criticism

Routinely assess the effect of your associations and joint efforts. Request criticism from the two players to evaluate the viability of drives and recognize regions for development. Valuable criticism fills in as an establishment for nonstop improvement and reinforces the drawn out suitability of associations.

6.2 Exploring Difficulties

Challenges are intrinsic in any cooperative exertion. When confronted with deterrents, move toward them as any open doors for development and learning. Address difficulties proactively, looking for transparent correspondence to track down arrangements. The capacity to explore difficulties decidedly adds to the flexibility of your associations.

6.3 Scaling Associations and Effect

As your organization grows and associations extend, investigate chances to scale your effect. Recognize ways of utilizing your aggregate assets, organizations, and ability for more extensive drives. Scaling associations includes extending existing connections as well as spreading out to shape new associations that line up with your developing targets.

6.4 Observing Accomplishments

Praise accomplishments, achievements, and imparted triumphs to the associations you interface with. Acknowledgment and affirmation add to a positive working relationship and prepare for future joint efforts. Openly perceiving the effect of cooperative endeavors likewise features the worth of associations with a more extensive crowd.

1. **Finding Local Therapy Cat Programs**

   Treatment feline projects have earned huge respect for their positive effect on people's psychological and profound prosperity. While treatment canines have for some time been the essential concentration, treatment felines are progressively ending up important friends in different settings. In this investigation, we dig into the universe of nearby treatment feline projects, looking at their starting points, benefits, and the special jobs these catlike colleagues play in improving the personal satisfaction for people confronting different difficulties.

Authentic Viewpoint:

The idea of treatment creatures traces all the way back to the late eighteenth century when creatures were first perceived for their capability to give solace and friendship. Nonetheless, treatment felines acquired conspicuousness all the more as of late, with formal projects arising in the late twentieth 100 years. These projects at first centered around canines, however as the restorative advantages of felines became clear, a shift happened, prompting the foundation of nearby treatment feline projects.

Advantages of Treatment Felines:

The advantages of treatment felines are complex and stretch out across different segment gatherings. Not at all like their canine partners, felines are known for their free yet loving nature, making them reasonable allies for people who might lean toward an all the more serene and unpretentious type of treatment. Research shows that connections with treatment felines can lessen pressure, lower circulatory strain, and work on generally state of mind, making them important in medical care, instructive, and local area settings.

Medical care Settings:

Nearby treatment feline projects have tracked down a critical spot in medical care settings, where the presence of these catlike sidekicks has been connected to worked on understanding results. Emergency clinics, nursing homes, and recovery focuses have embraced treatment felines as a painless and savvy method for advancing mending. The relieving presence of a feline can establish a quieting climate, offering comfort to patients managing different ailments.

Instructive Conditions:

In instructive settings, treatment felines add to making a positive and comprehensive environment. Schools and colleges have consolidated treatment feline projects to assist with reducing pressure during test periods, give solace in directing meetings, and improve the general prosperity of understudies. The non-critical and harmless nature of felines makes them especially successful in cultivating consistent encouragement for people exploring scholastic difficulties.

Local area Effort:

Past conventional establishments, treatment feline projects assume a significant part in local area outreach. These projects frequently collaborate with nearby associations to give solace and pleasure to people confronting affliction. Whether it's meeting covers, public venues, or fiasco stricken regions, treatment felines have a remarkable capacity to interface with individuals on an individual level, offering friendship during troublesome times.

Treatment Feline Preparation and Accreditation:

One critical part of effective treatment feline projects is the preparation and confirmation of these catlike colleagues. While felines are normally natural, explicit preparation guarantees they can explore different conditions and answer fittingly to a scope of circumstances. Certificate processes change however for the most part incorporate evaluations of personality, socialization, and fundamental compliance abilities. Nearby treatment feline projects team up with proficient mentors to guarantee that their catlike members satisfy the guidelines important to give compelling treatment.

Difficulties and Contemplations:

In spite of the various advantages, treatment feline projects face difficulties and contemplations. Sensitivities, anxiety toward felines, and likely disturbances in specific conditions are among the worries that coordinators should address. Furthermore, guaranteeing the government assistance of the treatment felines themselves is central, as the requests of treatment work can burden. Neighborhood programs should figure out some kind of harmony between offering important types of assistance and focusing on the wellbeing and joy of the catlike members.

Examples of overcoming adversity:

Accounts and examples of overcoming adversity from people who have encountered the beneficial outcomes of treatment feline projects are instrumental in featuring the meaning of these drives.

Individual accounts frequently underscore the significant everyday reassurance given by treatment felines, representing the effect these projects can have on emotional wellness, social cooperations, and generally speaking personal satisfaction.

Neighborhood Drives and Organizations:

The outcome of treatment feline projects frequently depends serious areas of strength for on with nearby networks, organizations, and medical services suppliers. Neighborhood drives can incorporate associations with veterinary facilities, pet stockpile stores, and volunteer associations to guarantee the maintainability and development of treatment feline projects. Such associations offer monetary help as well as add to bringing issues to light about the advantages of treatment felines inside the local area.

The Eventual fate of Treatment Feline Projects:

As the attention to the advantages of treatment felines keeps on developing, the eventual fate of nearby treatment feline projects looks encouraging. The joining of innovation, for example, virtual treatment feline meetings, may extend the compass of these projects to people who can't get to them face to face. Besides, continuous examination into the restorative impacts of creature helped mediations is probably going to give extra proof supporting the extension and coordination of treatment feline projects in different settings.

2. **Volunteering Opportunities and Requirements**

Chipping in is a respectable and caring method for adding to the improvement of society while acquiring individual satisfaction. Across the globe, there are different open doors for people to chip in their time and abilities, each with its extraordinary arrangement of prerequisites. This guide expects to dive into different chipping in open doors and the related requirements, offering experiences to those anxious to have a constructive outcome.

Understanding the Range of Chipping in Potential open doors

1.1 Neighborhood People group Commitment:

One of the most available and effective types of chipping in is inside the nearby local area. Open doors flourish, from helping at nearby food banks and sanctuaries to partaking in area tidy up drives. The prerequisites for such open doors frequently rotate around an eagerness to commit time, energy, and an enthusiasm for local area administration.

1.2 Instructive Drives:

Chipping in instructive settings can gigantically reward. Potential open doors incorporate coaching understudies, coordinating extracurricular exercises, or tutoring youthful personalities. Necessities might fluctuate, for certain projects looking for people with explicit subject skill or an overall obligation to cultivating learning conditions.

1.3 Ecological Preservation:

For those enthusiastic about the climate, chipping in preservation projects offers an opportunity to have an immediate effect. Whether it's tree planting, ocean side clean-ups, or untamed life conservation, chips in frequently need a veritable love for nature and a readiness to take part in genuinely requesting undertakings.

1.4 Medical care and Human Administrations:

Chipping in medical care and human administrations includes offering help to those out of luck. Amazing open doors range from working in clinics and centers to aiding eldercare offices. Prerequisites might incorporate historical verifications, essential clinical preparation, and a sympathetic nature.

1.5 Catastrophe Help and Compassionate Guide:

In the midst of emergency, volunteers assume a significant part in giving guide and solace. Amazing open doors in catastrophe help include quick reaction to cataclysmic events, and necessities might incorporate crisis reaction preparing, actual wellness, and the capacity to work in testing conditions.

Key Prerequisites for Chipping in

2.1 Age and Lawful Contemplations:

Age limitations are normal in certain chipping in open doors, especially those including minors or particular errands. A few projects might expect volunteers to be of a specific age to follow legitimate guidelines or guarantee the security of every elaborate party.

2.2 Time Responsibility:

Understanding the time responsibility required is fundamental while considering chipping in open doors. A few jobs may just request a couple of hours out of each week, while others, particularly those in worldwide or catastrophe help, may call for a more huge time speculation. Imminent workers ought to evaluate their accessibility everything being equal.

2.3 Abilities and Capabilities:

Chipping in valuable open doors frequently require explicit abilities or capabilities. For example, showing English might require capability in the language, while development activities might require volunteers with applicable specialized aptitude. Evaluating individual abilities and adjusting them to the prerequisites of the open door is significant.

2.4 Historical verifications:

In jobs that include working with weak populaces, for example, kids or the old, historical verifications are a standard necessity. Associations need to guarantee the security and prosperity of those they serve, and volunteers might have to go through screening processes prior to reaching out.

2.5 Preparation and Direction:

Many worker programs give preparing or direction meetings to furnish volunteers with the fundamental information and abilities. This is especially normal in jobs where explicit methods should be followed, like medical services or calamity alleviation. A guarantee to partaking in such meetings is much of the time an essential for contribution.

Finding and Applying for Chipping in Potential open doors

3.1 Nearby Worker Associations:

Local area based volunteer associations are brilliant beginning stages for those hoping to get involved locally. These associations frequently team up with different drives and can direct people to open doors that line up with their inclinations and abilities.

3.2 Internet based Volunteer Stages:

Various web-based stages associate workers with associations out of luck. Sites like VolunteerMatch, Optimist, and For Great permit clients to look for open doors in light of area, interests, and abilities. Making a profile and effectively looking for potential open doors is a proactive method for finding chipping in jobs.

3.3 Philanthropic Organizations:

Straightforwardly reaching charitable organizations is one more successful method for investigating chipping in open doors. Numerous associations effectively look for volunteers and value people contacting express their advantage. Organizing with philanthropies in areas of individual energy or skill can open ways to significant open doors.

3.4 College and School Projects:

Understudies can use college and school programs that work with chipping in open doors. These projects frequently team up with nearby associations and give an organized system to understudies to take part in local area administration.

Tending to Difficulties in Chipping in

4.1 Adjusting Responsibilities:

Volunteers might confront difficulties in offsetting their chipping in responsibilities with different obligations. It's essential to evaluate the time responsibility everything being equal and discuss any imperatives with the chipping in association. Finding an equilibrium guarantees supported inclusion and forestalls burnout.

4.2 Social Responsiveness:

For those participated in worldwide chipping in, understanding and it is fundamental to regard nearby societies. Volunteers might experience social contrasts that require liberality, flexibility, and an eagerness to gain from and team up with the networks they serve.

4.3 Taking care of oneself and Staying balanced:

Chipping in, while satisfying, can interest. It's significant for volunteers to rehearse taking care of oneself and lay out solid limits. Staying balanced guarantees that volunteers can support their responsibility over the long haul, proceeding to have a constructive outcome.

www.ingramcontent.com/pod-product-compliance
Lightning Source LLC
LaVergne TN
LVHW010342200726
843507LV00010B/1616